THE
GARDEN *at*
HIDCOTE

THE
GARDEN
at
HIDCOTE

FRED WHITSEY

PHOTOGRAPHS BY TONY LORD

F

FRANCES LINCOLN LIMITED

PUBLISHERS

Frances Lincoln Ltd
4 Torriano Mews
Torriano Avenue
London NW5 2RZ
www.franceslincoln.com

CONTENTS

MAP

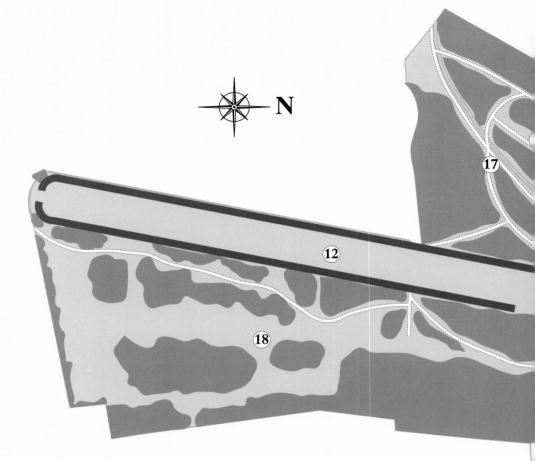

N

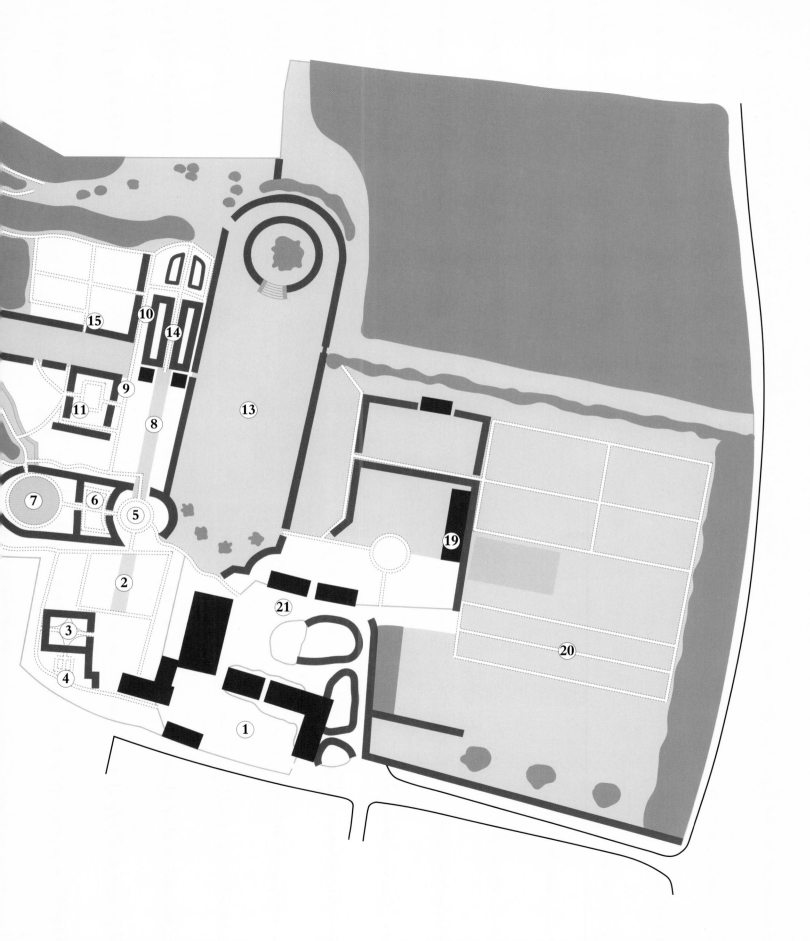

PROFILE *of the* GARDEN

No garden made in the twentieth century has had a greater influence on the evolution of the art of garden design or home garden making than Hidcote Manor Garden. None has more clearly charted the direction the style of gardening has taken in our time. None has offered more vivid inspiration to garden makers in their use of architecture with plants and in arranging relationships between them so that one enhances another. Hidcote's influence lies heavily upon gardens made in the latter half of the twentieth century – irrespective of their size and whether those who have made them realize it.

Small by some standards, large by others – it covers 10 acres/4 hectares – Hidcote is a successful fusion of many elements. Within its scope it embraces the broad sweep of the landscape architect's vision. At the opposite extreme is its multitude of incidents, even details that are fussed over. It offers countless moments of fascination to 'plantsmen', those gardeners who are won by the lure of plants as individuals. Seen from a different perspective still, it is the work of an artist using plants as his palette, the earth as his canvas. In essence Hidcote reconciles all sorts of gardening interests and persuasions, whether they are passionate or pernickety, artistic or botanical, bold and extrovert or of an intimate nature, whether they spring from castle or cottage.

On its chilly hilltop on the northernmost spur of the Cotswold hills, Hidcote can therefore be seen from several standpoints. Its first attribute is its firm design. Here again this is the meeting place of several elements. Of widely disparate derivation, they are nevertheless brought together to create an easily identified whole with a distinctive personality.

The garden has dramatic vistas that exploit the largest possibilities of the site. It even 'borrows' the views of the surrounding countryside in the manner of the great eighteenth-century landscape gardens, which were divided from their distant environment only by a ha-ha or sunken boundary – a component which Hidcote has as part of its extremities.

In the French style it has tall hedges screening a boscage and creating a vista that seems to stretch into infinity. Also showing French influence is its box-edged parterre of intricate design, with a planting scheme that changes with the seasons. Echoing some Italian gardens, it has a suite of 'rooms', one leading into another and only sparsely furnished with plants. In character with an important era in the development of the English garden it has a streamside garden and a series of mysterious woodland glades that meet, interlock and turn away from one another, inviting one to explore them further.

The Great Alley, the 'spine of the garden', is composed of a progression of episodes and leads to a view across the Vale of Evesham, but this is not revealed until the visitor reaches the escarpment. (Even a fox's curiosity can be aroused.)

The colour theme of the Old Garden is worked in soft tints enlivened by flashes of pale yellow. Every opportunity for exploiting a vista is grasped.

Deep borders of hardy flowering plants there are, ample in proportion. They are of the scale that graced the home gardens of the wealthy Edwardians and that were a reaction against the sumptuous Victorian carpet bedding, which seemed as if the greenhouse had been moved outside for the summer. Hardy herbaceous plants also occur in a group of compartments that often seem to visitors like the rooms of an endearing, welcoming country house. As you progress from enclosure to enclosure, all of them contained within walls sometimes of brick but more often grown from yew or holly or beech, or sometimes all three, you are constantly teased into discovering what lies behind the next opening. The cunning use of surprise – one of the most potent stratagems in the landscape designer's art – becomes a matter of astonishment here. Above all, Hidcote has tousled cottage garden borders that, for all the garden's sophistication, link it directly to the surrounding Cotswold villages which help form its natural environment. It is the areas planted like this that make it most easy for visitors to relate Hidcote to their own experience and to the garden at home. For these flower borders are small scale, even intimate.

Jumbled though the borders seem at first glance, their confusion is contrived and an illusion. In truth they are composed with an art that conceals art; the apparent disorder is actually a pattern. Their scheme has two strong interwoven threads, each of which each has an independent existence, like counterpoint in a work of music.

First is the grouping for colour effect. No plant that is not related in colour to its neighbours has a place. Usually the effect depends upon blends rather than on

contrasts, though not slavishly. In one area where the general level is a soft blend of pinks and mauves in many tones, the scheme is lit by flashes of moonlight yellow and silver. By contrast on a bold scale, the colouring can be dramatic, as in the celebrated twin red borders, one of the most daring enterprises in the whole of garden making.

Running concurrently with the theme of colour is that of succession. Everywhere always seems full of plants in flower or significant shapes. At no point in the gardening year, from the end of March till the early days of November, does an area of Hidcote fail to make an impact. So artfully is its planting conceived and carried out that as one grouping of plants goes over and retires into the background another takes the stage. By studying this element alone the visitor to Hidcote can learn many lessons in garden making.

So skilfully, too, are the plants arranged that a huge collection is employed in the overall scheme. The planting could have been done with many fewer kinds, but the man who created this garden was clearly a collector animated by a wild passion for acquiring and growing different plants. The collection is one that could have been assembled only over a lifetime of gardening. Trees and shrubs, bulbs and what are known as rock plants, roses and climbing plants are all used lavishly. Few annual flowers appear – only the odd patch added here and there to strengthen a summer effect. For this garden is really an essay in the exploitation of permanent plants. In addition to the framework provided by the hedges, there is an enduring structure of trees and shrubs. This is coloured in

Making a sharp contrast, the central episode along the Great Alley is an assembly of 'hot' colourings, set off by purple, copper and bronze foliage plants.

with herbaceous perennials, which die down in autumn and reappear with the spring; these make the strongest contribution of flowers. Bulbs pierce their undergrowth and frequently they are interplanted with carpet-forming plants and overhung by the arching branches of shrubs that are essential to the composition.

The garden even has its terraced beds where grow the true alpine and silver-leaved plants that need a site from which rain drains away swiftly, and which would not otherwise survive a winter. At the opposite extreme there is a collection of waterside and water plants, which enjoy having to spend all their days with their roots in mud and would not grow anywhere else.

Although the soil is naturally alkaline, the Cotswolds being limestone hills, Hidcote also has its lime-hating plants, which extend its horticultural horizons still further. Rhododendrons and camellias grow in sites specially created for them.

Roses grow everywhere, though there is no rose garden; they are part of every planting scheme throughout the garden. Rarely are they the varieties customarily pruned back hard every year: rather they are climbers and roses developing into shrubs and allowed their heads, even if sometimes they need the support of a framework of posts to enhance their display. Again, in the number of different kinds grown, never confined to an area of their own but always set in close company with other plants, the roses help to make the garden one that bears the stamp of someone's zeal for collecting. As for lawn, there is a vast one, like an auditorium. The architect again.

And so Hidcote, besides being a National Trust garden to enjoy as part of the British heritage as one would a country house, is a gallery of plants, a superbly arranged one, but also a textbook on garden making. Its plantings serve as a model for realizing that romantic ideal of an 'all-the-year' garden, which offers its beauty no matter what the day or the month. It is in this way a dream made reality.

ABOVE The natural soil in the southernmost border in the Old Garden was dug out and replaced with a mixture congenial to lime-hating plants.

OPPOSITE Lawrence Johnston, creator of Hidcote, followed a policy of dense companion planting, as in this section of the scene through the Rose Borders.

The MAN BEHIND the GARDEN

So imaginatively conceived, brilliantly inventive and lavishly planted as Hidcote is, it inevitably invites the question: what sort and condition of man was the person who made it, who brought together so many ideas and executed them with so deft a touch? Efforts to piece together enough material for a biography of Lawrence Johnston, and to discover the man behind the garden, have been made several times, but they have usually faltered, for there are large gaps in what can be discovered about his life. Equally, the sources of his inspiration lie hidden. He remains an enigma, someone who defies being pinned down by the curious like a butterfly in a collection. While his garden is so exuberant, so distinct a statement, the only picture it is possible to build up of him is one of a man who shunned the limelight and public knowledge and was secretive to the point that now, many years after his death, he is as elusive as thistledown. It is a fate he would have welcomed and perhaps chuckles over in the shades.

What is known of the life of Lawrence Waterbury Johnston, though it was a very long one, can be simply told. He was born in Paris on 12 October 1871, of wealthy American parents. Where did the money come from? Here it is necessary to explore a little genealogy. Lawrence Johnston's father, Elliott Johnston, born in 1826 at Baltimore, Maryland, came from a family engaged in the world of banking but also of social standing. Elliott had a brother, Henry, who married a lady called Harriet Lane. She was the great-niece of James Buchanan, fifteenth President of the United States, who followed Abraham Lincoln. In his earlier days James had been the United States ambassador in Britain. Before marrying, Harriet had acted as his hostess in London.

Elliott Johnston, Lawrence's father, married Gertrude Cleveland Waterbury, daughter of an industrialist, in 1870. Her grandfather had also been in banking, and her father, Lawrence Waterbury, was in the cordage industry, making not only rope and binding twine but manilla paper and material for wrapping cotton. It can only be a matter of speculation why the couple were living in Paris at the time of Lawrence's birth, but much of his boyhood was spent back in New York, where Elliott died in 1884. Three years later Gertrude made a second marriage, to a successful lawyer named Charles Winthrop. Sadly, Winthrop too died after only a few years of marriage. Gertrude inherited substantial sums of money from her father and each of her

Although the Manor House is seen from the garden from many angles, curiously it stands unrelated to the garden, its windows commanding no direct view of any area.

The Old Garden is bounded by a wall, a relic
of the days when it was the Manor's kitchen
garden. Now it is richly draped with climbing
plants such as this spring-flowering
Clematis montana var. *wilsonii.*

husbands. Her second widowhood and the loss of two other children in the family left
mother and son close and she, as outgoing as he was retiring, became the dominant
figure in his life.

Johnston's education was placed in the hands of a tutor and together – mother, son
and tutor – 'they wandered', in the words of one of his later friends, though no one
knows where their travels took them. No word of Johnston's early life and experiences
ever fell from him in the hearing of any of the contemporaries it has been possible to
question. He took the Roman Catholic faith, while his mother retained her New
England Nonconformism.

Quite early he seems to have merged into Englishness, though he always retained
links with France. As he entered manhood he either developed a wish to go to an

English university or it was put to him that this was the course his life should take. But he was unprepared for the classical road and in order to acquire the necessary entrance qualifications he had to study under a crammer. He was twenty-three before he entered Trinity College, Cambridge, and he graduated in history in 1897. Soon he was to take out naturalization papers and become a British citizen.

Whatever intentions he had then about embarking upon a career, if indeed he had any, and what efforts he made in following one, were interrupted in 1900 when, having enlisted in the Imperial Yeomanry, he went off to South Africa to serve in the Boer War. It is hardly likely, given what little we know about his character, that he intended to make the army his calling, though he retained the title of major to the end of his life. Soon after he came home he was farming in Northumberland in the company of a friend – a life very different from that one might expect of a son of wealthy American parents domiciled in Europe. One could reasonably guess that he had developed an inclination for the rugged rather than the plushy life into which he was to settle later.

In 1907 he became an English country gentleman, a Cotswold landowner with a windy hilltop estate of 280 acres/113 hectares. The estate consisted of a hamlet, a farm and a gentrified farmhouse known as 'the Manor'. His mother paid for it and the two settled there together, a wing being added to the house for his occupation. Johnston was then thirty-six. With one interruption, Hidcote was to be his total preoccupation and his career for almost the next half century.

Very soon, he developed an expansive taste for gardening, if this had not already been gestating within him during the years of which little is known. He indulged it with energy and extreme gusto. He began with almost nothing save the unremarkable, even hostile site. The only features it had were a Lebanon cedar, squat rather than soaring, and a clump of beech trees, with two more a little way off. The land looked towards the west, tilting slightly upwards as it receded and obscuring the hilltop view from the house. It took a steeper fall to the south-west and dropped abruptly over a short patch of ground south of the house, which was narrowly bounded by the first cottage of the village. It was chilled by the air from the open north and swept by the prevailing winds from the south-west. And the soil had lime in it. It was hardly the place where anyone with experience of gardening and knew what he was about, who also had wealth, would choose to make a garden. That the opportunities with which he began were so meagre greatly enhances the achievement.

Over the next half-dozen seasons, employing the money his mother allowed him and manifestly a great deal of hard labour, Johnston designed, levelled on a vast scale and planted exuberantly. He created compartments and vistas. He laid paths and set out hedges, some traditional, others innovative. A series of photographs that were taken as soon as 1913 show that by then the 'suite of rooms' had been built and furnished. So far as is known he drew up no formal plans; the evidence is that he worked by simply pegging out his ideas on the ground. Soon he became more ambitious still: with the vision of a latter-day Le Nôtre he strode out into the country, taking his garden to the extremities of the hilltop.

What was the inspiration of his ideas? No one knows. Possibly memories of places he had visited during the family's 'wanderings'; perhaps illustrations in books. It is tempting to fasten on the latter theory. Several seminal works on the development of gardens were published around that time, some related to the work of the Arts and Crafts movement, practitioners of which were active in nearby villages. He cannot have been unaware of the movement and nor can it have failed to make some impact on him. From what is known of the way he worked in the garden he was later to make in the south of France, the likelihood is that he kept his hand on every detail. Besides, there are amateurish touches – clear evidence of improvisation. Johnston has been said to have had an architectural training and these improvisations also prove this to be one of the fictions that have grown up about him.

Working in England at that time were several professional garden architects with well-established practices, whose names are now imperishably enshrined on the history of gardening. Prince among them was Edwin (later Sir) Lutyens, who was always ready to design gardens appropriate to the houses he was building. But Johnston consulted none of them. He relied upon his own eye and instinct. My own conjecture, though, is that his handbook was a book called *The Art and Craft of Garden Making* by the landscape architect Thomas H. Mawson, which came out in 1900 and went through five editions in the next twenty-five years.

The year 1914 put a stop to it all. He rejoined the army and fought in Flanders, this time in the Northumberland Fusiliers. He was wounded, gassed and once mistakenly left for dead. No sooner was the war over than he was back at Hidcote, working at its restoration after the four years of neglect and developing the garden still further. Then began its great days. The hedges had grown up, the trees had soared and the aspect of maturity had begun to settle over the garden. The dreams of the earlier years were becoming reality. And Johnston's love for his garden was becoming a consuming passion.

In 1922 he engaged his first head gardener, a man of outstanding ability and zeal. Frank Adams came from a line of professional gardeners and had been trained in several important gardens; he had returned from the war to take up a job as a flower decorator at Windsor Castle. He was thirty-two; Johnston was now fifty.

The horticultural sympathies of the two meshed. Johnston was the visionary, Adams the practical man who had the job of realizing the flashes of inspiration – and often putting them into a realistic perspective. In the manner of numerous head gardeners and their masters before him, he became his master's confidant.

Johnston had remained unmarried. Adams had brought with him to Hidcote a wife and young daughter. The day's work over, evening after evening the two men were closeted in the Major's study 'up at the Manor', discussing projects and progress – to the chagrin, in time, of Mrs Adams, who saw less and less of her husband as he became infected by his employer's overmastering enthusiasm for the garden and gave everything he had to it.

Meanwhile, Mrs Winthrop, alarmed at the scale of her son's spending on the garden, confided in Mrs Adams that she feared he was 'a waster'. Sometimes the purse strings were pulled back. It was within her power to do so, for she never made over to him capital in the United States. She did not even bequeath it to him at her death. He remained her dependant and later that of her trustees.

Adams gathered round him a team of gardeners who quickly picked up the spirit of the place and became imbued with the enthusiasm that dominated Hidcote then. 'You couldn't avoid it,' recalled one of them, Charles Wigmore; 'it was infectious.' 'The most exciting time of my career,' said another, Jack Percival, son of a famous head gardener, later to rise to a similar position himself. 'I still wish I had been able to go back and work there again after I had moved on to "better myself".'

Johnston's most formative years horticulturally were those when the writings of Gertrude Jekyll appeared in *Country Life* and *The Garden* and when her books were being published. It is more than likely that he read them, but it is not known that the two ever met. Most of the worthies of the world of horticulture then clustered round the Royal Horticultural Society, and he was among them. He was elected a member of the Garden Society, the most exclusive gardening club in the world, membership of which – by invitation only – was restricted to aristocrats who gardened expansively on their estates. Every year his head gardener, as Johnston's proxy, would go up to London to the Chelsea Flower Show, staying several days in order to make repeat visits. Yet no mention of either Hidcote or its owner ever appeared in the RHS *Journal* until the year when he handed over the property to the National Trust. This is in key with the rest of the Hidcote paradoxes, and with what is known or can be inferred of Johnston's character.

What was he like, this man whose life's work has made so prominent a landmark in the chronicles of gardening but whose own place in that history is so blurred?

Physically he was slight and only 5 feet 8 inches/1.7 metres tall. He was fair and blue-eyed. Usually he dressed in the garb of a country gentleman of his time, in knee breeches and leggings, and later in the fashionable plus fours and hose. Always there were spaniels at his heels, later a family of dachshunds. He spoke quietly in the measured accents of the English upper classes but pronounced his 'r's in the swallowed French fashion. His eyes were distant and abstracted when he looked at anyone, but so shy was he that in spite of his military career and rank, and his experiences of camaraderie with other men in battle, he seldom made a direct relationship with anyone. Most people who met him found him studiedly courteous but distant.

The evidence is that he was a man of extreme reserve who revealed nothing of himself to anyone. To those who knew him in his later years, at the time usually for recalling and reflecting on the past, he never reminisced about any period of his own earlier life. He kept no diary to which he confided his thoughts and experiences, only an engagement book. As a letter writer he was laconic rather than loquacious.

Unusually for a man of his social standing – he was, after all, lord of his little manor – he took no part in local affairs. It was his mother who took an interest in the little village community, visiting each family every Sunday before lunch. If he was ever invited to sit on the bench he declined. He was, however, a keen tennis player and at times engaged a coach, whose tutoring was available to his house guests. He also played squash and turned one of the old farm buildings adjoining the courtyard into a squash court, though later this was sacrificed to some of his potted tender plants, becoming their winter quarters.

As to whether in the later days of Hidcote he ever did any practical gardening himself, no former gardener he employed whom I have spoken to ever saw him working with his hands. In any case, had he wished to, the canons of propriety that ruled in a private garden in those days would have forbidden it.

Relations with his garden staff were courteous and amiable rather than concerned or involved. On his daily rounds of the garden he would talk to his men – there were usually five working under Frank Adams – about the work on which they were engaged. While the head gardener was always 'Adams' to him – more out of a respectful comradeship than seigneurial dignity – it is significant that he broke with the convention of the times and always called all the others by Christian name, as though they were members of a family team, with whom he might have known a closer relationship but for the reserve he could not escape. 'He may have been remote to strangers,' said Jack Percival, 'but he was very friendly to his staff: we would have done anything for the Major at Hidcote.'

His household was presided over by a butler, Thomas Merrill, and more commandingly by his wife Margaret, the cook-housekeeper. He kept a fine table and entertained frequently, filling the house with extravagant arrangements of flowers from the garden of his own work. He was as fastidious about his food as he was about every detail of his garden. Besides maintaining the cellar, Merrill had to be certain they never ran out of Vichy water, for like a Frenchman of his day, Johnston never drank from the tap. The hospitality he dispensed was mannered and exquisite.

Who were his friends? What company did he keep, this reclusive well-heeled bachelor who did not set out on his life's adventure till he was nearing middle age and whose consuming passion was now in full flood? Rarely were they people with no interest in gardening. 'Besotted' with the subject himself, as he has been described, and single-minded, he naturally sought the society of those who could discuss it, if not at his level then with erudition.

Most influential was Norah Lindsay, an artist with plants who went from house to country house advising the titled and the moneyed on the development of their gardens – and combining plants so that their colours merged and the foliage gained its deserved importance. Her lasting memorial is the parterre garden of perennials facing the east front of Blickling Hall, in Norfolk, another National Trust property, where the planting schemes she devised are maintained. She had a garden of her own not far from Hidcote, the Manor House at Sutton Courtenay in Oxfordshire, where Hidcote-like Irish yews stood among rich plantings of perennials.

Another friend, who entered his life later, was Mrs Heather Muir, his nearest neighbour, who from 1937 onwards was making a garden at Kiftsgate Court at the end of the short lane that leads to Hidcote. She and Johnston exchanged not only plants but ideas too. Mrs Muir was a woman of acute artistic sensibilities whose own garden was carefully colour schemed, as though the plantings were the furnishings of a room.

Down at Broadway the American actress Mary Anderson de Navarro, a well-connected socialite, lived in a superb stone property and gardened with élan, as did the eccentric Charles Wade at Snowshill Manor, now also a National Trust garden and house. In the other direction, at Stow-on-the-Wold, was a man named Mark Fenwick, who was surrounding his Abbotswood home with a garden, more masculine in this case, that has retained to this day the renown it gained then. Another of his gardening associates was the Hon. Robert James, who at Richmond in Yorkshire created a garden in which its outlines were also opportunities explored to their utmost limits and where shrubs, hardy perennials and low-growing plants and bulbs were the raw materials.

More women were members of his circle of friends, though, than men. He clearly enjoyed the society of women, to whom he was a courtly figure, but there has never been any suggestion that any of them were anything more than friends. He was flattered by their admiration for his artistry, which they recognized more readily than his men friends, who tended to be 'plantsmen'. Johnston combined the two roles.

Through the two pre-second war decades, however, Johnston seems to have had one male friend with whom he constantly discussed the development of the garden, Lord Barrington. He was one of the three men who shared the home of Mrs Violet Gordon Woodhouse, the celebrated clavichord player of the time, with her husband, at Nether Lypiatt Manor, near Stroud, where Norah Lindsay was also a frequent visitor, according to Sir Osbert Sitwell in his memoirs. Sitwell also recalls the life of this household in detail, but in his account Johnston's name receives not a single mention.

A bust of Major Lawrence Johnston, in the custody of the conservators of his other garden in the south of France.

Another friend, a Bostonian who had settled in France, was the American novelist Edith Wharton, whose novels evoke the wealthy Boston society, rigid in its codes, to which Johnston's parents belonged. Johnston helped her make both the garden round the former monastery she leased at Hyères on the Riviera and the garden at the Pavillon Colombe, near Paris, a Louis XV villa on the edge of the forest of Montmorency. In her diaries she refers to him many times as a visitor and companion on nursery visits in the south of France, which they often made in the company of the younger Vicomte de Noailles. She stayed at Hidcote several times, describing it as 'tormentingly perfect'. She described Johnston as 'angelic' and declared, 'He helped me incalculably in all my planting plans.'

Inexperienced in the wider world though Johnston may have been, and generally ill at ease with people outside his own social milieu, he was however fond of children, and indulgent towards them. When Frank Adams's daughter was ready to convalesce from a serious illness at the age of nine, he packed her off in her father's care to stay for six weeks at his Riviera villa. The three Muir daughters at Kiftsgate were his friends and as they grew and became better swimmers he had the pool at Hidcote, to which they had an open invitation, extended and deepened at one end so that they could learn to plunge. For their mother he applied his artistic gifts to painting the ceiling and frieze round the wall of Kiftsgate's largest room in the Italian style. After the paint was dry he enlisted the help of the three girls to rub it all over with boot polish to 'antique' it and the four worked together distressing it for three days.

Painting was the one other pursuit besides gardening that Johnston followed. He frescoed the wall of the thatched house by the bathing pool, but his work is now almost obliterated by weathering. He painted the domes of the twin gazebos, and in the north one four Chinese vases are seen against a blue starlit sky above a marbled frieze. One of his flower pieces hangs in what is now the tea room, and his magnum opus seems to have been two views he painted of the Red Borders, which he hung in his bedroom. In the earlier Hidcote days Johnston had a studio at one end of the tender plant house that stood just south of the kitchen garden overlooking the pool there. But this too ultimately gave way to playing the role of orangery for his growing collection of tender plants, housing them over the winter.

Tender plants were to have another setting in Johnston's gardening life. By the early 1920s the skeletal form of Hidcote had been fashioned so distinctively and its plantings so clearly defined that he could leave it for long periods in the hands of his sympathetic head gardener and turn his creative talents to other territory. He chose a winter retreat on the French Riviera just north-west of Menton, in the Val de Gorbio, and there he began to garden with the same imaginative zest he had brought to his chilly site high up on the Cotswolds.

Here at Serre de la Madone Johnston would spend the winter months. He had another team of gardeners to look after it all, led by one of his English gardeners. The garden was one of wild extravagance where he attempted to grow every plant he came across that might enjoy the shelter.

As he reached his sixties, having designed and 'painted' his two masterpieces, Johnston now added the role of plantsman to that of garden artist. He fell into a thraldom with plants. Like a possessed gambler, he bought and planted everything he

The farmhouse which Lawrence Johnston extended and made his home in the Val de Gorbio, Menton, on the French Riviera. Named Serre de la Madone, it looks towards the south-west and stands at the head of a series of some twenty terraces, each with its own characteristic planting scheme.

could lay his hands on. It was the era when the fruits of the great plant-collecting expeditions to the Far East were becoming available, giving a strong impetus to plantsmanship among those who had space and wealth. By this time Johnston had established contacts at the Royal Botanic Gardens at Kew – when he visited he was taken round by the curator, the celebrated W.J. Bean – and he was subscribing to the great plant-hunting expeditions. Many of the plants that came to prominence then were species that would suffer no lime in the soil and the Hidcote land had plenty. No matter: he would change it in parts of the garden that were appropriate. The plants he provided for in this way were shrubby, and meeting their special likings made it possible to give them a companion groundwork of woodland plants with similar needs.

This man of catholic horticultural tastes was busy, too, on alpine plants, which became fashionable in the 1920s. The two-tier terrace garden below the southern boundary of the Great Alley was built specially to grow plants that would not flourish outside a sharply draining site.

The frameyard that lay between the Pine and Slab Gardens and the tennis court was the centre of intense activity. Hundreds, if not thousands, of pots of sown seeds, each with an asbestos cover to exclude light and retain moisture, stood there, sunk in beds of sand retained by railway sleepers. It was somebody's job to watch over them for the first signs of germination, to keep the soil at the right degree of moistness and raise or lower the covering frame lights according to changes in the temperature. Johnston's lust for acquiring more and more plants for the garden had become insatiable. He had also fostered close connections with the Royal Botanic Garden Edinburgh, and between the years 1923 and 1940 he received from there seeds or growing stock of as many as seven hundred plants for his propagating programme.

Quite early in his gardening career Johnston established several principles for himself. 'Plant only the best forms of any plant' was primary. 'Plant thickly' was another, in the knowledge that where the gardener doesn't put a plant nature will: 'Pack them in,' he would say to his gardeners as he watched them at work. A third was 'Compose plantings from all types of plants' – even, on a temporary basis, summer-flowering annuals besides the framework of trees and shrubs and the underplantings of hardy perennials.

Graham Stuart Thomas, Gardens Consultant to the National Trust for many years, described the garden when he visited it in the 1930s in its glory days:

> There would be one plant climbing over another, a group of disparate shrubs united by a continuous under-planting of some lowly flower; there would seldom be a single clump of any herbaceous plant or bulb, rather would it be grouped here and there creating the effect of its having sown itself; the colours were and are mostly blended to separate schemes with occasionally a deliberate clash. Seldom is one plant given one whole piece of ground; it shares it with others. All this hangs together because of the firm design, which is so much enhanced by the vertical lines of dark evergreen hollies and holm oaks.

Much has been made of Johnston's own plant collecting expeditions but these reveal his enthusiasm more than an achievement. There is no record of any discovery of his coming out of his 1927 visit to South Africa. He went in the company of Captain Collingwood Ingram and Reginald Cory. Joining the party when they got there was the botanist Dr George Taylor, later to be knighted after he had become Director of Kew Gardens. They were a strangely assorted group: Ingram, an amateur naturalist, impulsive and irascible; Cory, amiable and an active man of business, used to getting things done; Taylor, dour, learned and suffering no fools; and retiring Johnston, whose only interest was his gardens and who had brought along his valet to look after him. In Ingram's autobiography, in which he recounts something of the trip, Johnston's part gets a mere handful of lines in the story of his calling to stop the car because they had just passed a plant 'of superlative beauty' that they must at all costs collect. They stopped and saw, high up, the crimson 'bloom' of what appeared to be a liliaceous plant that needed treacherous handholds to reach; it proved to be no more than a piece of red paper blown there.

Johnston's visit to western China in 1930 in the company of the highly experienced collector George Forrest, who worked for the Royal Botanic Garden Edinburgh, with the support of private patrons, was a more ambitious and greatly puzzling venture. Johnston was by then almost sixty, a man with a damaged lung and inexperienced in such demanding work. How did Forrest, who had previously worked alone in those distant forests and fast ravines, and trained a large company of native collectors who could be trusted to continue the work in his absence, come to accept such an unsuitable partner? Forrest, though small in stature too, was a man of powerful strength who had been trudging the Yunnan mountainsides at intervals for twenty-five years. So iron-like was his physique that in the days when he had worked at the Botanic Garden he walked six miles each way to and from his home and stood all day in the herbarium. Something the two men had in common, though, was reticence: Forrest talked little and wrote down no more than he had to.

The expedition had its ugly side. Johnston got ill. The two quarrelled. Forrest came to dislike his companion, even despise him. In one of his reports to the Director of the Royal Botanic Garden Edinburgh, Professor William Wright-Smith, he wrote: 'Had I raked G.B. with a small tooth comb I couldn't have found a worse companion than Johnston . . . Johnston is not a man, not even a bachelor, but a right good old spinster spoilt by being born male.' It is not surprising that Johnston, an aesthete who, though possessed by a mania for collecting plants, would never add one to his garden if it would not enhance the picture, had to give up and return home. Will Ingwersen, a Serre head gardener who had been on many alpine plant collecting expeditions since boyhood, tried to draw Johnston on his experiences in what was one of the world's more fertile sources of new garden plants, but he failed: Johnston was evasive and would recount nothing of them.

Nevertheless, whether because of Johnston's help or not, the expedition proved to be one of the most successful ever undertaken. In a letter home Forrest wrote: 'I expect to have nearly if not more than two mule-loads of good clean seed, representing some 4–500 species, and a mule-load means 130–150 lbs . . . If all goes well I shall have made a rather glorious and satisfactory finish to all my past years of labour.' The purpose of the expedition had been to get seed of plants missed on his previous expeditions or collected by others and now lost, or of those that had not germinated or been in short supply. Forrest spent most of his time organizing from his base at Tengyeuh, fifty miles or so from the border with Upper Burma, and it was near there that seed of *Mahonia lomariifolia*, one of the plants most associated with Johnston and later to become the parent of a race of hybrids, was collected. He appears to have taken it to Serre de la Madone, from whence he distributed plants and where it has now become naturalized. Another species of this genus, *M. siamensis*, with orange flowers, was also collected and a plant of it has survived for decades at the Serre. It proved frost tender elsewhere, though at the Cambridge Botanic Garden – to which many of the plants at the Serre were sent after Johnston's death – it has crossed with *M. japonica* to produce the large-leaved 'Cantab' hybrid, which has been found to be hardy. The third plant of which seed went to the Serre is the well-known *Jasminum polyanthum*, now sold as a winter pot plant in hundreds of thousands. It had first been discovered in 1883 by Père Jean Marie Delavay, a French missionary, and Forrest had found it again in 1906, but it was not until Johnston started giving friends plants from the Serre that it gained any recognition.

The name Lawrence Johnston has become properly associated with two garden plants: a form of the South African *Verbena peruviana*, always used in the Hidcote Red Borders for its bright cherry-red flowers, and a rose. The verbena was noticed at the Serre garden in 1938 by C.P. Raffill, then curator of Kew Gardens, when visiting there,

and brought back to England and named. It gained the Royal Horticultural Society's Award of Garden Merit in 1948. The rose, a yellow climber, was bought as an unnamed seedling from its raiser, Joseph Pernet-Ducher of Vénissieux, near Lyon, in France, a sister seedling of the better-known 'Le Rêve', introduced in 1923. At first it was called 'Hidcote Yellow', but it was later named by Graham Thomas 'Lawrence Johnston' with his consent, under which name it received the Award of Garden Merit in the same year as the verbena.

The authenticity of attaching the name Hidcote to some of the other plants that bear it is open to question. Mrs Diany Binny, one of the Muir girls, who later took over running Kiftsgate Court garden from her mother, recalled hearing Albert Hawkins, once the Hidcote vegetable grower, who had charge of the whole garden in the early post-war years, being asked about various plants and glibly giving the answer, 'Oh, that's the Hidcote so and so,' more out of pride than botanical exactitude. Inevitably, though, in such a richly planted garden sports arise as oddities on established plants, marriages are made by natural forces and produce hybrids, while plants seed themselves.

As the thirties advanced Hidcote matured and rose to its supreme days. But it remained a closed, private world; rarely was it open to the public. Strangers who had heard of it were not welcomed. Two heavily illustrated articles appeared about it in *Country Life* in 1930, and Russell Page, later to become one of the world's most eminent garden designers, described its wonders in a talk broadcast in 1934, which was reproduced in *The Listener*. But Johnston still remained in the background, though receiving the plaudits of the cognoscenti.

The war clouds began to gather and the skies darken. Like the nip of autumn, unease entered the air. Johnston was now in his middle sixties. He had reached an age when contemporaries began to leave. His mother, with whom he had spent so many close years, had been gone more than ten years. His creative zeal had run its course. He had created two works of genius. Hidcote's boundaries were set; at the Serre the terraces flowed into one another as the plants prospered. He remained held in thrall by his gardens but he had begun to receive intimations of mortality. Frank Adams, who had been widowed and had married again – receiving as a wedding present from the Major three months' sojourn at the Serre villa – had had several nasty attacks of illness, and Johnston was moved to confide to him that if anything should happen to him he did not feel he would be able to go on with the garden. The spell was showing signs of vulnerability. The bell poised in its little turret on the courtyard chapel roof was sounding a call to vespers.

Late in 1939 Adams died. And war began. At the outbreak of the war Johnston was away in Menton at his winter retreat, his other demi-paradise, and soon he found himself trapped there. As the German forces moved through France the English community left on the Riviera were in a state of alarm and resolution: they must get home. Johnston was among them as they made their way along the coast to Marseilles, leaving behind their villas, their possessions and their dreams of a sunlit evening to life. They boarded a coaler without berths or comfort, perilously overloading it, and after days of misery and anxiety at sea, but thankfulness at the chance of reaching home, they arrived at Falmouth.

In the warm southern climate of the Riviera, and less often in sheltered borders at Hidcote, *Mahonia lomariifolia*, one of the plants brought back from Johnston's 1930 expedition to western China, fruits periodically.

For five years Johnston carried on at Hidcote with what limited help he could get. For so labour-intensive a garden it was in good order again when in 1948 he was persuaded that it was of such significance that it must be preserved and that the best chance of that would be in the care of the National Trust. Hidcote was the first garden to be brought into the Trust's custody. It was a signal moment in the Trust's history. Although so few had ever heard of Hidcote and fewer still knew it, its fragility and outstanding originality underpinned the realization that other gardens of great importance were likely to be in danger and would need preservation. So a joint Gardens Committee of the Trust and the Royal Horticultural Society was set up, with Hidcote its initial charge, soon to be joined by the great Bodnant in North Wales.

The previous year Johnston had been awarded the Royal Horticultural Society's Veitch Memorial Medal 'for his work in connection with the introduction and cultivation of new plants'. Making the presentation – to a cousin of Johnston's, standing on his behalf – the Society's then president, the second Lord Aberconway, called him 'a great artist in designing gardens at Hidcote'. He continued:

> There has been no more beautiful formal garden laid out since the time of the Old Palace of Versailles than that designed on quite a small scale, but with exquisite artistry, by Major Lawrence Johnston. Not only that, but the garden is filled, as the earlier gardens were not, with interesting and beautiful plants, some of which he has himself collected in the mountains of China. No one better deserved the Veitch Memorial Medal than our old friend Major Lawrence Johnston.

Not long afterwards relatives of Johnston's from the United States who had never seen their British kinsman before visited him in his home. He received them with the same quiet courtesy for which he had always been known, but they found him a confused old bachelor, deeply troubled with a sense that the most cherished thing in his life was no longer his. Finally, taking the dachshunds with him, and in the care of his valet and his wife, Alfredo and Maria Rebuffo, he went off to the Serre, returning two or three times in the early days but then coming back no more. On his last visit to Hidcote he commented that opening to visitors 'spoils the pleasure of a garden, which should be a place of repose and to get away from this world'. Then it was open only three afternoons a week and a mere 3,500 came in a year. Today that figure approaches 150,000.

The haze of Johnston's confusion thickened and he sank into death in 1958 at the age of eighty-six. He was brought back and buried beside his mother in Mickleton churchyard, near Hidcote. Characteristically their graves lay apart from all others there. In his will he left his modest estate in England of £2,922 to friends and employees, and sums for the maintenance of the Catholic Church at Chipping Campden and for masses to be said. The family portraits, including one of his great-great-grandfather's second wife, who, the will said, was the first white child to be born in Baltimore, were to go to the Maryland Historical Society but it declined the bequest.

'He was a genius,' said Kew's director, Sir George Taylor, of Johnston. 'A very great man,' said Charlie Wigmore, a former gardener at Hidcote, 'who never got the recognition he deserved.' 'Hidcote has influenced me more than any other garden,' said

Russell Page, at the pinnacle of his profession. Single-minded, private, concentrated, obsessive, besotted – Lawrence Johnston has been called all these things. Yet we know little of what led him into this state of possession, what influences played upon him, what animated him; he was remote, shy, retiring, reserved, committing nothing to paper, confiding no thoughts or feelings. 'It was three months before he hardly spoke to me after I went to work at the Serre,' said Will Ingwersen, 'and then I found I really liked him.' 'A little dormouse of a man,' said James Lees-Milne, a National Trust official who had a hand in the acquisition negotiations and who had met him in boyhood. 'I knew Johnnie Johnston for thirty years,' said the Vicomte de Noailles, who for more than a generation stood at the centre of French gardening and was a most shrewd and sympathetic observer of the human tragicomedy, 'but I never *knew* him.' Perhaps Lawrence Johnston was really a man who lacked powers of self-expression save through his gardens. Perhaps the quest for the real Johnston need go no further than their pathways and alleys.

Like the nave of a great cathedral, the avenue of Huntingdon elm trees, now felled and replaced with Turkey oaks, looked to the north, across the vale of Avon.

$\mathcal{T}he$ GRAND DESIGN

Hidcote's overall layout is complex, its components and incidents diverse. It is a garden in which the visitor must get a clear mental plan. Otherwise you are led to wander this way and that, stopping repeatedly as you encounter some unfamiliar plant and ponder, until you have lost any sense of direction and have strayed far from the unifying main walk on which the whole garden is built.

When the Manor House had its addition built on, a new entrance door was made in a corner of the Courtyard (1), somewhat unprepossessing, but with a carved tablet of armorial bearings set into the lintel. It is through here that visitors are received. You walk through rooms, in which are displayed photographs of some of the scenes the visit will reveal, and out into the garden by way of the Manor's original main door. Immediately you find yourself in a richly gardened area, small but suggesting the many delights to come.

To either side of the steps down are plantings of one of Hidcote's main signature plants, the famous violet-coloured lavender. Your curiosity is stirred: clearly you are in the presence of unfamiliar and exciting prospects.

Against the walls are bushes of *Azara microphylla* in its variegated leaf form. In February its flowers may not seem very significant but their scent is – definitely it is of vanilla. A cousin bush, *A. serrata*, stands in a corner where two walls join. Also of South American origin, it is larger in its May flowers and its foliage. Another South American, *Acca sellowiana*, which has fluffy mimosa-like blooms and edible berries, embellishes another wall. In the foreground is a grouping of a south European, *Teucrium fruticans*, with blue flowers the summer long and enduring foliage that suggests the plant's origin with its silvery undersides. This handful of plants helps to suggest the nature of this great and highly individual garden and the richness of its multitudinous plantings.

Before you lies what has been called the Great Alley, the heart of the garden from which all else radiates. This is a thrilling, exultant moment. In the theatrical quality of the vista, its use of perspective, it might be compared with the permanent stage set for Palladio's theatre at the Italian city of Vicenza, centre of that designer's main work. Fortunately there is a centrally placed seat on which you can sit and take it all in. Before you reach out the arms of the old cedar.

As the visitor makes his way towards the distant gate and viewpoint, the incidents that make up the Great Alley are revealed area by area, as in this opening to the Circle.

The Stilt Garden, just beyond the twin pavilions, is not fully revealed until the visitor reaches the flight of steps up to the platform on which the pair stand.

Very soon you realize that though the vista is continuous, running through what seems several hundred yards, it is actually composed of several elements. The land rises a little, needing a flight of steps in the far distance. As the view recedes, the hedges and trees are set closer in, creating a false perspective and thus lengthening the view by illusion.

Immediately in front of you lies a panel of grass running between twin borders. You are in what is still called the Old Garden (2), the first area to be developed after Johnston took over the garden. Here the planting, though luxuriant, is in soft colourings lit by patches of silver and moonlight yellow. A gateway in wrought iron links walls to either side and hesitatingly seals off what lies further on, yet reveals something of it. Just beyond are some crossing paths in brick that seem to follow arcs rather than straight lines. The turf continues to run between two more flanking borders, this time planted with nothing but red and orange flowers and purplish foliage. Then comes the flight of steps. On each side at the top of these stands an elegant little pavilion in light rose-coloured brick, each with a silvery-toned ogival roof.

The pavilions are set off by the square heads of what can be seen from their clean trunks to be a pair of pleached hornbeam plantings, between which the linking grass

path continues. Beyond is a pair of tall gate piers in brick, each capped by a bust thrown into relief by tall yew hedging. The wrought ironwork of the gates forms a pattern against the sky, to which the whole scheme leads.

Though this view is well known, having been pictured in countless books, and on thousands of calendars, mugs and table mats, the reality is so stirring that you rise almost in relief from your position on the seat and take a little path to the south. You find yourself in a small enclosed garden, having exchanged grandeur for intimacy. Beyond lies yet another little garden reached by an ungated opening.

The first (3) is the White Garden (formerly the Phlox Garden), planted entirely with white flowers and plants with silver foliage. Dark green pieces of topiary rise from the box edging that fringes the stone paths. Purple-leaved Japanese maples dominate the adjoining enclosure, the Maple Garden (4), where a rectangular central flower bed is outlined in box. The surrounding borders of shrubs and perennials are raised and the soil is retained by low brick walls. The design is formal, the plantings loose and permanent.

Take a curling path leading out from the south-east corner of this enclosure and you will find that it brings you to the point where a stream enters the garden but soon disappears out of sight into a culvert. Later this will reappear, broaden and

Formerly a garden devoted to summer-flowering phlox, the White Garden is dominated for many weeks by the rose 'Gruss an Aachen', long cherished at Hidcote.

BELOW Edged with the 'Munstead' strain of lavender, the Circle has a ring of the rare Rouen lilac.

OPPOSITE The Circle is a pivot of a secondary axis, the first section of which is the Fuchsia Garden. In spring this has a dense planting of blue *Scilla siberica*.

become a major feature. Here is one of several shady borders made up with lime-free soil and supporting a community of acid soil-loving plants, notably some of the smaller-leaved rhododendrons. Now follow a right-angled path – you can take no other here – which brings you round to the gate leading from the walled Old Garden to the second incident that makes up the Great Alley, called simply the Circle (5).

This is in fact, as you quickly discover, a little garden of its own, based on a series of concentric circles described in brick and plants. Immediately in front, on its western radius, it looks towards the Red Borders running up to the twin gazebos, but the southern radius reveals it to be a pivot on which a crossing axis with three more circles hangs. This first section is a small parterre, the Fuchsia Garden (6), where the box-hedged beds are indeed thick with fuchsias during the summer. Beyond, between a pair of topiary peacocks clipped in yew that rise above a low box hedge, is the Bathing Pool Garden (7), with a huge circular pool raised to waist height like a tank in a Spanish garden. Overlooking this, on slightly higher ground still and beyond the pool, is a handsome pedimented arch clipped in yew. This leads into a third enclosure, also based on a circle. It proves to be a further surprise, for

An incident encountered suddenly and unexpectedly during a tour of the garden is this tunnel of lime trees. At its southern end is a balustrade from which can be enjoyed a view of the area known as the Wilderness, planted for autumn colour.

it is empty of plant furnishings, an untenanted *cabinet de verdure* such as you find closing some of the lesser vistas at Versailles.

At this stage you could be led into further diversions, such as the small enclosure to the left, where stands a thatched loggia with carved oak stanchions, or to take one of the inviting paths that lead into what is obviously woodland. Having done so, return for a moment to the keynote of the garden, the Great Alley. Only to find, however, that having established your position again there are more diversions beckoning.

After taking a closer look at the Red Borders (8) from here, where the colouring appears more startling still, follow a little path to the left and you will discover that parallel with this section of the Great Alley is a broad path running for a full hundred yards and focused on a splendid urn set off by a tall yew hedge at the end. It has on one side an area planted with ferns and other shade-loving plants under

tall ilex trees. Opposite is the Winter Border (9). Next, running southwards at right angles, comes a tunnel of lime trees made to arch over a short path with a balustrade at the end. This looks over an area on a much lower level, over a section of the stream where the banks are thickly planted with ground coverers and some of the shrubs that are part of the rich assembly of the Stream Garden. The end part of the path you must still follow, though, has on its north side what is called the Alpine Terrace (10). This consists of two tiered beds filled with alpine plants and dwarf shrubs.

But before you reach this, again to the south of the broad path you are following now, is a hedged enclosure reached by narrow openings, the area called Mrs Winthrop's Garden (11) for Major Johnston's mother. Here the colour scheme with which it is planted is worked in blue and yellow flowers and foliage. This commands a concentrated and highly contrived view over the Stream Garden and through a

Named Mrs Winthrop's Garden in honour of Lawrence Johnston's mother, this enclosure is planted with blue and yellow colourings.

series of grassy glades lying to the south. It looks across a low-lying area watered by the stream where the waters discharge from the conduit that ran somewhere under the three circular gardens. On a marshy patch a family of flamingos once strutted, contributing to the decorative scheme. The picture has been composed with many kinds of trees and shrubs, and in the far distance white-stemmed birch trees seem to sit on the horizon. All is artfully schemed to frame the longest possible view skywards.

To keep your bearings, you would do well to resist the temptation to take one or other of the paths that descend to the stream and instead return to the Great Alley by way of the Red Borders. You go up the steps and first admire the Delft tiling that decorates the northern gazebo and the domed ceiling frescoed by Major Johnston. Then you turn to the opposite gazebo on the south side and once again you are transfixed. It stands on an eminence commanding a dramatic view along the Long Walk (12), one of the most surprising in the whole garden and again one of the most notable in the history of garden making. A simple avenue of turf is hemmed on either side by tall formally clipped hornbeam hedges that run the entire length, severe, a huge empty box about 200 yards long and 4 wide. The uncompromising parallel lines of the hedges appear to converge as they recede, combining with the vast stretch of turf to give a sense of calm and spaciousness.

Rising from behind the hedges are teasing glimpses of an assembly of trees that from the diversity of their foliage must be of special horticultural interest. But again the invitation to explore must be resisted for the moment.

The inclination to pass through an opening in the yew hedge just behind the north gazebo, however, might be given way to for a moment. It leads to the Theatre Lawn (or Great Lawn) (13). This is a refreshing and sobering moment after so many heady experiences passed through on the way. The area is huge and uncluttered by vegetation save for the clumps of trees at either end.

Across the lawn is a broad opening in the northern yew hedge, leading to a soberly planted beech wood. There are more French overtones here. A wide beech allée runs severely through it and at the end, as an eyecatcher, is a fine pair of timber gates. But once more it is the sky that seems the real point of focus.

By this time the prevailing spirit of Hidcote will have established itself firmly and the southern influences will have been seen all around. It is revealed to be a garden where warmth has been coaxed and contrived – with the shelter of its hedges, the comforting intimacy of its enclosures and the singular, sizzling plantings of the Red Borders at the heart of the garden. And always it is to the south of the site that one is coaxed to explore, not the chilly north.

After this calming diversion, return to the platform between the gazebos, two-thirds of the way along the Great Alley. From here, looking back towards the point where you first joined it, you receive the full force of this startling composition again. The green of the Circle makes a background for the exciting originality of it. Beyond the Circle the twin borders of the Old Garden, planted so delicately in their pale colourings, make that seem farther away than perhaps it is. Always there is the spreading cedar, standing in its off-centre position.

From this point you now realize, as you turn back towards the western extremity, that the 'boxes' that, behind the gazebos, threw them into relief in the first view of that dramatic scene, are hornbeams trained formally in the French fashion, their trunks bare, their heads pleached to turn them into boxes on pillars. This is the Stilt Garden (14). Further still towards the western end of the complex scheme is another section, again an unsuspected incident: a pair of beds hedged in by balustrades of yew with silver-headed pampas springing from them.

These stand on the highest ground in the garden, where the soil is retained by a high wall. On a lower level to the south you can see more enclosing hedges still and a series of tall clipped yews peeping above them. Steps and openings lead down into the Pillar Garden (15), another of Hidcote's most photographed areas. The name comes of course from the surprising set of pillar-like yew trees planted formally here. The ground plan is heavily patterned with a geometric system of crossing paths, leading to a central panel of turf. Though it has been levelled, some of the

Of French inspiration, this allée of tall beech trees stripped of their lower branches looks towards the north but has, as an eyecatcher, a pair of timber gates made to a design illustrated in one of Gertrude Jekyll's books.

paths still fall away to the south. Each path has its own predominant plant that lines it. The effect of these is to strengthen the geometry and add boldness to an area that might otherwise be fussy. But it is the pillars that give the garden its main theme.

It is almost a secret garden this, bounded on two sides by tall hedges, on a third by a belt of trees and on the other by a great heap of soil like a prehistoric burial place. In the absence of records of the garden it must be assumed to be composed of the soil from the levelling that was done here. It has been turned to good account into something of a rock garden. One side, that facing east, is coated with scree as it might be in nature. On the others are outcrops of rock.

Beyond all this, on the western slope of the hilltop on which Hidcote was created, called the Bulb Slope (16), the horticulture still goes on, though more landscaping now than gardening. The view from here is expansive and inspiring, eventually reaching into Wales. A ha-ha divides the escarpment that looks to the west from fields where cattle graze, and where farmland and orchards clothe the land that falls gently into the distance. On the horizon, a little to the left, lies the sprawling hump of Bredon Hill. Seen further away, across the Vale of Evesham and looking just a little north, is the tip of the Malvern Hills. Strategically sited parkland trees frame and concentrate each view.

On fine days the soft white clouds carried by the winds from the south-west lazily help compose great open skyscapes. When the weather is stormy they become violet-black, sweeping in with terrifying relentlessness. If you stay on in the garden late into the evening you may see one of the brilliant sunsets that expire only with the slowly unfolding darkness. One day sheep may safely graze in the foreground; on another it may be a herd of cows, munching as they stare at you as though only they had the right to be there.

Leaving this splendid prospect, from here you take a course a little downhill to the left, going past the boulder-strewn bank set with overgrown squat shrubs and through a glade in which the occasional maple stands surrounded by a carpet of turf. The interlude gives relief from the prevailing sense of enclosure and exuberant planting. Such alternations between openness and confined areas heighten the effect of each section of the garden and distinguish it from those old gardens

Daffodils are planted lavishly in the Pillar Garden to give a bold spring effect.

from which Hidcote takes its inspiration, which were composed entirely of a series of interlocking courts.

Going south from the Bulb Slope, you soon pick up one of the stone-faced paths that allow comfortably dry walking right through the Stream Garden (17). From the belt of trees, their fringe overhanging a bridge that crosses the stream, you quickly emerge into the open again. Look to one side towards the fields and another view of the surrounding country opens beyond a lower section of the ha-ha that sweeps round the western boundary of the garden.

Without such pauses it would be a restless experience coming here. For though unified by a characteristic spirit, the garden has so many openings in hedges and walls and one after another invite you forward. Together with the contrived views towards the sky these moments of repose also serve to make you look up and outwards from time to time in a garden that is intricately patterned with plants that would otherwise claim your constant attention.

Now you are at the foot of the Stream Garden, its lowest point. From here the paths run uphill to the east. It follows the course of the stream that, on your left, runs between steep banks. They are thick with plants whose nature it is to enjoy having their roots in mud. On the higher ground there is a rich assembly of shrubs, well spaced to allow room around them for herbaceous plants that have grown into dense carpets. Lilies rise from among them at intervals, which give these a chance of showing off their graceful deportment.

At its topmost point the Stream Garden, now broadening, meets the Long Walk just where it dips and begins its gentle rise to the great gates away on the southernmost extremity, framing the sky. Look left and there stands the south gazebo on its platform. You follow the southward course of the Long Walk but soon an archway on the left cut in the hornbeam 'wall' begs you to stray from the way you have chosen. At once you find yourself in an area completely different from anything the garden has shown you so far.

This way and that, a system of glades runs between plantings of shrubs that in turn are overhung by trees, some gaunt and showing silver or ashen trunks, others multi-stemmed and spreading rather than soaring. We are in the part once dubbed Westonbirt and named the Wilderness (18) today, planted primarily, like that other great Gloucestershire garden after which it was named, for the display of finery it puts on for the lingering weeks of autumn. This principal theme has been preserved, but its beds have been given a collection of hardy shrubs, chiefly hydrangeas for summer and herbaceous plants with leaves that contribute to the autumn pageant.

Now you are wandering inside the view seen as a distant prospect back in Mrs Winthrop's Garden, close to the Great Alley. Between the white-stemmed birch trees on what seemed then the horizon spreads a panorama of farmland, coppices and open hilltops patterned by dry stone walls characteristic of the Cotswolds, right away to where the distant line of the Cumnor Hills meets the sky.

Look back in the opposite direction into the garden and your eye passes through the glades, over that damp area where once the flamingos paddled on unbelievably fragile legs but now filled to choking point with plants that will have nothing but moisture permanently about their roots. There in the distance are the carefully

clipped hedges of the more formal parts of the garden, the seats either side of the opening to Mrs Winthrop's Garden standing out in relief against them.

Beginning the return journey, follow the broader glade beneath tall trees of rhus, maple and sorbus, and make for the area through which the stream runs, still keeping to the east of the Long Walk. Now the banks are broad rather than steep and planted with a dense groundwork. Still there is an upper layer of shrubs and above them tall ilex trees, giving the impression of a miniature forest belonging to a southern land.

Many kinds of hydrangea have their home here, none more striking than the velvety-leaved *Hydrangea villosa* in a large plantation devoted to it. Yet another stone-faced path leads immediately to where the hedged enclosures began. At once you enter the flowerless *cabinet de verdure*. You are back to the view that encompasses the Bathing Pool, the Fuchsia Garden, each on a different level, and then the Circle. It is framed by a pedimented arch cut in yew mingled with box. This is a moment, too,

Berry-bearing shrubs and trees chosen for their hectic leaf colouring in autumn make a brilliant finale to the garden's year in the Wilderness.

Lawrence Johnston had a deep delight in birds and maintained a small flock of flamingos, providing them with a special pool and sheltering night-time and winter quarters.

to note the colouring of the hedges that enclose the Bathing Pool and then the Fuchsia Garden. In one case the matt yew is enlivened with the highly polished leaves of holly; in another holly, copper and green beech are grown together to make the famous 'tapestry' hedge.

Take a side exit from the 'green room', and you are invited to follow a quadrant-shaped path leading through a gap in an old wall to the Italian House. In front is the bathing pool and round to one side are steps leading up to the Fuchsia Garden between the topiary peacocks. Three more steps take you up to the Circle.

Then to your left opens again the splendid view of the Red Borders, the tilted roofs of the gazebos outlined by the heads of the pleached hornbeams beyond. Between them is that framed view of the western sky again. The view in the opposite direction is dominated by a powerful silhouette of the cedar and the stone house behind it. In front of them lies the softly coloured Old Garden, as gentle as a watercolour.

Now cross the Circle and go out by the north-running path that crosses the eastern end of the Theatre Lawn and passes an area devoted again to beds of alpine plants – the Pine and Slab Gardens – including some of the greatest treasures set in old stone sinks raised up on piers. In a moment you see the splendid Plant House (19), and then go on along the twin Rose Walk (20), planted to either side in the manner of most of Hidcote's flower borders. Return, admiring the roses and other plants on the opposite side, and go back to the Garden Yard (21), and then through the shop into the main courtyard again.

The circuit of the garden is completed and you are ready to get to know intimately the plants with which each separate area is furnished. Their numbers are vast, their variety adventurous, the touch with which they are used as sure as it is inspired.

Integrated into the overall scheme, the bathing pool is raised to waist height in the manner of pools in many Spanish gardens. This area has some of Hidcote's finest topiary. The peacocks pre-date the Second World War.

The COURTYARD

If the two main entrances to Hidcote, marked by pairs of engraved stone gate piers capped with finials of classical design, give the Courtyard (1) a certain grandeur – though the gates are of painted timber rather than ironwork – the plantings are loose and even random, lacking the formality that might seem appropriate. A carriage and pair could turn in it with a little coaxing, but in truth it is hardly a manorial courtyard, and asymmetrical instead of studiedly formal. Its origins are humble. Once, before the house was elevated in status, this was the farmyard. The first pair of gates are set diagonally across one corner of the broken rectangle. The handsome

The main entrance gates, their piers capped with fine finials, are set at an angle to the quadrangle that is the Courtyard, which was fashioned from the farmyard of former days. The little chapel in the Courtyard (BELOW) was created from an old farm building. Never consecrated, it is now used for exhibitions.

buildings immediately opposite were adapted from the byre that held cattle, and that on the right was once the great barn, where their fodder would have been stored for the winter months – often severe on this wind-swept hilltop.

Even the little chapel is converted from a farm building. It still has the flight of outdoor steps leading up to its hayloft, and the unchanged disposition of the building means that though it has been dignified by being given a window with stained-glass fragments set within decorated mullions, this looks to the north, not the east. The chapel remained part of a dream: it was never consecrated and today it houses an exhibition. The whole complex represents a transformation from something basically rural in character to one belonging to an elegant country residence, yet at once personal to its owner.

The gate piers have not been left untenanted by plants. Swagging one is the Rambler rose 'François Juranville', recognizable from its highly polished copper-tinted leaves and its flattish flowers with quilled petals that open coral and fade to soft pink. At the other entrance one of the piers is embellished with another Rambler, the purplish 'Violette' – a singular rose, since its parentage has always remained unknown and it is one of the very few thornless roses.

On the wall separating the Courtyard from the lane grows the rare climber *Schisandra rubriflora*, a Himalayan species carrying crimson flowers that hang like little lanterns of waxen texture. The first shrub you meet is a nursery hybrid, *Osmanthus × burkwoodii*, a lusty grower with many small white flowers in spring that have a summer perfume of privet. Close to it grows a spreading clump of the red-hot poker *Kniphofia caulescens*, greyish in leaf and with thick stems that loll on the ground like serpents asleep and flowers that change from coral to pale yellow.

Now comes one of the garden's greatest glories: its most famous name plant, *Hypericum* 'Hidcote'. This semi-evergreen bush has provoked great argument among botanists. Legendary attributions vary from it being a plant raised in the garden itself to it being imported from Mount Kilimanjaro in Kenya. All that is certain about it is that it has ancestors in China and is a highly attractive hybrid plant, carrying its well-shaped golden flowers from June till well into October and flourishing anywhere.

Another hybrid close by from the same stable as the osmanthus is *Viburnum × burkwoodii*. This has in it the blood – and the perfume – of the celebrated *V. carlesii*, but is much more vigorous and has a longer flowering season, which begins in January and continues until May. There is an aged plant here of one of the very finest of all the hardy fuchsias, 'Mrs Popple', with crimson and purple flowers that could rival those of some of the indoor fuchsias. It was discovered in a garden near the former Six Hills Nursery in Hertfordshire and given the owner's name by the nursery's proprietor, Clarence Elliott, an alpine plant specialist and one of Johnston's gardening friends.

The walls of the chapel are dressed with fine plants. There is one of the slender-growing Alpina *Clematis* 'Blue Bell', flowering in spring. The west-facing wall is draped with one of the climbing hydrangeas, *Schizophragma hydrangeoides*, a plant that grows in Japanese woodlands as honeysuckle does here. Its show of 'flowers' is really one of bracts – a device of nature's to attract fertilizing insects – which appear cream at first but take on a pink hue as they develop and mature. At its feet grows

Hidcote's most celebrated name plant, the famous *Hypericum* 'Hidcote', which, appropriately, has a prolonged flowering season.

Two noble frost-tender shrubs flourish in a sheltered corner of the Courtyard: *Mahonia lomariifolia*, which flowers in November, and *Magnolia delavayi*, grown principally for its magnificent foliage.

another of the 'Hidcote' name plants, the famous compact lavender, which we shall see planted more expansively in the Pillar Garden.

On the corner is another of the hybrid shrubs raised by Albert Burkwood when he was a member of the Burkwood and Skipwith partnership at their Kingston-upon-Thames nursery in the early 1930s. A longer stayer than either of its parents, *D. caucasica* and *D. cneorum*, *Daphne* × *burkwoodii* has retained the characteristic scent in its pale pink clusters of flowers. Near by, enjoying the shelter of the sunny west wall, is one of the garden's few successful plantings of the South African *Nerine bowdenii*, which produces its 'frosted' pink lily flowers in October. A small plant of the Californian creeping blue blossom, *Ceanothus thyrsiflorus* var. *repens*, has long endured in this bed.

Crossing the Courtyard to the north-east corner, you find one of the plants Johnston was responsible for introducing from his 1930 expedition to western China: *Mahonia lomariifolia*, a lanky evergreen bush with sprays of yellow flowers that open in November. It has been given one of the garden's most sheltered corners, which once had a glass overhead covering; the brackets that held the purlins supporting the glass can still be seen. These are of the type familiar in Victorian kitchen gardens for protecting the choicer types of plums, peaches and apricots grown against south- and west-facing walls. Such was Johnston's particular gardening bent and overriding concern, however, that the system was employed to shelter supposedly tender ornamental plants, not food crops.

This mahonia has played an important role in the development of its genus, for it became a parent of a series of evergreen shrubs that flower in winter and can contribute architecturally to gardens throughout the year with their fine evergreen holly-like foliage and splendid poise. *M. lomariifolia* itself proved to be tender, but its children suffer nothing of this weakness. The first of them, named *M.* × *media* 'Charity', arose as a chance seedling in a batch of *M. lomariifolia* cross pollinated with *M. japonica*, having occurred naturally in the former Slieve Donard Nursery at Newcastle, Co. Down, in Northern Ireland, where its proprietor, Leslie Slinger, had been trying, unsuccessfully, to procure hybrids between the two. The name mahonia recalls an interesting Irishman, Bernard McMahon (1775–1816), who left his native country to settle in Philadelphia. There he set up a nursery and seed shop where botanists and other horticulturists would gather. His reputation grew to such an extent that President Jefferson handed over to him seeds from the collecting expeditions he supported.

Another plant of doubtful hardiness grown here, originating in the same western Chinese region as the mahonia, is *Magnolia delavayi*. It is admired for its leaves, which are larger than those of any other member of this splendid leaved family of trees; evergreen, they can be 12 inches/30 centimetres long and half as wide. The flowers, however, are a disappointment: though the buds are large like the leaves, they release white flowers that are partly enclosed by green tepals (the technical name for parts of the magnolia flowers), which fade within a few hours of having opened during the night. In spite of the favoured site given it here, the Hidcote plant has been cut to the ground several times, the mighty tree being reduced to a few short sticks.

Two Frenchmen are honoured in the name of this noble plant, of which we shall find other examples elsewhere in the garden. Pierre Magnol (1638–1751) was the botanist director of the botanic garden at Montpellier. The species name commemorates the Jesuit missionary Père Jean Marie Delavay, one of the most successful plant hunters who, in addition to his ministry in China, collected plants devotedly and sent home to France over 200,000 specimens of more than 4,000 species, around 1,500 of them new to botanists. He contracted bubonic plague and became paralysed in one arm, but continued his work until his death at sixty-one in 1895.

The wisteria embellishing this wall is one of the several in the garden and the most magnificent of its kind, *Wisteria floribunda* 'Multijuga'. Its racemes of purplish lilac flowers can reach 24 inches/60 centimetres in length, though in its native Japan a plant was recorded early in the century by the plant collector E.H. Wilson (whom we shall meet in the Garden Yard) as having trusses more than 5 feet/1.5 metres long.

Another wisteria grows against what is now the garden's shop, the more familiar *W. sinensis*. Being in a sunny wall-backed site means that when it is in flower it receives sufficient warmth to release its powerful scent. At its foot grows the lavender that has been named 'Hidcote Giant' – giant in the size of its flower stems, which sometimes reach 24 inches/60 centimetres. Close to it an old

Every possible area is gardened – such as this pathway leading to the restaurant, where *Viburnum* × *juddii* and *Magnolia* × *soulangeana* 'Amabilis' have taken advantage of the shelter and grown to a large size.

yucca with spiky leaves and a developing trunk adds an architectural touch.

One of the most striking of the shrubs that adorn the walls of the shop is the Cape figwort, *Phygelius capensis*, in its deep red selection 'Coccineus'. It reaches to the eaves and through much of the summer is set with tube-shaped flowers, yellow in the throat, that immediately indicate its family relationship with the penstemon. It is South African in origin but has shown itself to be surprisingly hardy and to flower well without the sun.

Just here there is another bush with multitudinous weeping stems and leaves of a leathery texture. This is *Cotoneaster serotinus*, very rarely seen in gardens and a curiosity in its late flowering – it does not appear till July – and in its orange berries not ripening until well into the autumn. It contrasts markedly with the subtropical-looking *Fatsia japonica*, which has enormous glossy, five-finger leaves and carries heads of white flowers in the autumn and winter. At the foot here is the white Lacecap *Hydrangea macrophylla* 'Veitchii'. The term 'Lacecap' indicates the formation of two types of flowers comprising the head: fertile ones forming a cluster in the centre are surrounded by a ring of infertile ones attended by leaf-like bracts. This is one of nature's display devices to attract insects. We shall meet other Veitch namesakes in the Garden Yard.

Even in the kitchen garden, the 'business quarters' – in this case the staff canteen – are embellished with plants like this mighty example of *Wisteria floribunda* 'Multijuga'.

The OLD GARDEN

Essential to the Hidcote experience is the sensation of always being on terms of easy intimacy with plants; you seem wrapped around by them. This comes from the fact that almost all the flower borders are twins, each resembling its opposite if not being a mirror image, and the paths and vistas are driven through and between them. Only in two minor instances, the Terrace and the Winter Border, does the design depart from this principle. The effect is like that of walking through a bluebell wood or across a field of poppies. Thus despite the scenic features, the long vistas, the element of theatre, you always feel a participant, never merely a spectator. For want of an alternative, one talks of the garden's 'flower borders', but the term is scarcely appropriate. The 'walking through' experience is as different from watching a play staged 'in the round' as seeing it taking place beyond a proscenium.

Even in the heart of the Old Garden (2), perhaps the most richly planted section of all, where the twin plantings are divided by the broad panel of turf opening the dramatic scene of the Great Alley, you are still in direct contact with the work of the planter's hand.

To have made the plantings round the chief viewpoint in the Old Garden, from which the Great Alley is seen first and most often, anything but one bland in colouring would have weakened the theatrical impact of an avenue that strides out into the distance with incidents to be explored on either side. It would have distracted the eye at the start and lessened the powerful effect of the overall scheme. The colouring had to be soft and unobtrusive.

Thus it is pure Jekyllian and could be taken as the prototype of all those borders created in recent years with pink and mauve flowers lit by touches of silver and moonlight yellow. Unlike Jekyll's borders, however, it is carried out not purely in herbaceous plants but also with shrub roses, with a scattering of other shrubs and an underlayer of herbaceous perennials. In summer a few batches of annual and tender perennial flowers are brought out from the greenhouses and popped in to strengthen the colour and enhance the effect in those places where the tulips that provide spring flowers are dying down.

Large bays of tulips, renewed frequently for certain effect, open the season in the Old Garden while the bold plantings of hardy perennials are renewing themselves.

ABOVE, LEFT The full majesty of the ancient cedar tree, one of the few original features of the site, can be enjoyed from the vantage point at the head of the Great Alley.

ABOVE, RIGHT A careful choice of grass species has made it possible to carpet with turf the ground shared with the cedar – a site that would otherwise have been difficult to furnish – and links it with the turf panel running through the Old Garden.

Seen from the seat beyond the old cedar, the plantings look deep, extending into the lateral boundaries, and cunningly add to the sense of luxuriance, when actually they are threaded by paths which, as you discover when you explore, turn the area into four separate sections. One of these has a colour scheme distinct from the main area. Another at the southern boundary has an entirely different community of plants.

Rich, even lavish, though the scene which presents itself in the immediate foreground may seem all through the summer months, it is in fact composed of a great variety of plants so that on no day from spring to autumn is it devoid of colour. The relays come thick and fast in this splendid tapestry.

Dominating the scene to the left, as you look along the Great Alley, is a spreading little tree of rugged outline, bearing large white flowers in May and then strange russet fruits through late summer and autumn. It is tempting to think that this might belong to the pre-Johnston days, an echo of when this was the kitchen garden of a farmhouse. For it is a medlar – *Mespilus*

Astrantias, characterized by a 'starched ruff' underlying the inflorescence, form part of the groundwork for Hybrid Musk roses in the Old Garden.

germanica botanically, but as English in its history as a dog rose. It is one of the most ornamental of all flowering trees.

Many varieties of tulips open the flowering season. Then from the thickets of hardy perennials rise large old plants of the Hybrid Musk roses – varieties raised in the 1920s by a clergyman-turned-rose-breeder, the Reverend Joseph Pemberton, in his garden in the picturesquely named Essex village of Havering-atte-Bower. This umbrella name for them was later declared to be more fanciful than appropriate, since any trace of the musk rose in their ancestry is very far distant; however, the name has stuck. Giving a structure to the plantings, the representatives of this series here are 'Cornelia' and 'Vanity', 'Felicia' and 'Buff Beauty'.

Later-bred roses of the Floribunda type that are used are 'Lavender Pinocchio', 'News' and 'Mevrouw Nathalie Nypels'. Also here is a species as it comes from the wild, *Rosa glauca* (syn. *R. rubrifolia*), grown for the greyish green cast of its leaves.

Ingenious use is made of tall hardy perennials towards the west end of the southern border. The natural ground falls away and

THIS PAGE
ABOVE Multicoloured 'tapestry' hedges are among Hidcote's most distinguishing features.
BELOW, LEFT Most of Hidcote's ornaments are of horticultural origin. This figure clasping a miniature barrel is one of the very few exceptions.
BELOW, RIGHT Dahlias are some of the temporary plants added each year in the Old Garden to boost the summer display.

RIGHT
ABOVE This scene in the Old Garden vividly illustrates the technique of close planting, leaving little scope for weed growth.
BELOW LEFT, TOP AND BOTTOM Lilies are encouraged to grow up into companion plantings.
BELOW RIGHT Some plants are allowed to self-sow, adding to the sense of exuberance.

they restore the balance of the scene with their height. Among them are a bright pink spiraea called *Filipendula palmata*, the pink *Campanula lactiflora* 'Loddon Anna' and the blue *C. latiloba*. The last has sported in the garden to produce a lilac-pink form which has been named 'Hidcote Amethyst'.

The foreground shrubs include the cream-flowered *Potentilla fruticosa* 'Vilmoriniana', the cultivar name commemorating one of the most celebrated of French seed firms, so eminent that it once had its premises in the centre of Paris. Also contributing summer dabs of yellow is the Jerusalem sage, *Phlomis fruticosa*, one of the oldest of garden plants in this country. As summer begins to wane several kinds of phlox flower here, as does the faultless *Aster × frikartii* 'Mönch', one of the finest of all the hardy perennials which

carries its Michaelmas daisies from early August into October on a plant that needs no staking. A pink cornflower, *Centaurea* 'John Coutts', is notable here too, as are several kinds of ornamental grasses, all contributing as contrast plants. Also apparently indestructible in its length of flowering season is *Geranium × oxonianum* 'Claridge Druce', which spreads an evergreen carpet over the ground. In truth, however, more than a hundred different kinds of plants contribute to this tapestry-forming assembly.

Behind the main twin borders that comprise the first section of the Great Alley are the paths for the exploration of the flora of each.

The old wall to the north carries a plant of the yellow climbing rose given Johnston's name. Also growing against the wall are the fine honeysuckle *Lonicera henryi* and various

Rosa 'New Dawn' is trained to one of the Old Garden walls. Near by are bushes of the Hybrid Musk rose 'Penelope', trained to posts to give a plenitude of flower.

Foxtail lilies (*Eremurus* × *isabellinus* 'Cleopatra') and *Lilium regale* var. *album* partner one another in a sunny bed against the south wall of the house.

clematis, including the strange *C.* 'Alba Luxurians', which has small white flowers each with a sepal tipped with green.

A series of *caisses de Versailles* stand at the edge of the bed. In summer potted pomegranate plants – transferred temporarily from the greenhouse, where they are brought into bud – are plunged into them. When the flowers have expanded they are an exciting vermilion. For the spring the tubs are planted up with hyacinths.

Plants of foxtail lilies or *Eremurus* add tones of buff to this area early in the season, the flowers arranged in plumes that rise 5 feet/1.5 metres from the ground. At one time this area was composed mainly of blue and white flowers and there are relics of this scheme in the Michaelmas daisy *Aster* × *frikartii*, two species of *Ceratostigma* and the clear blue *Salvia uliginosa*.

If you were to take the transverse path at the top of the main borders here you would pass a bed where a hardy cyclamen from the Apennines, *Cyclamen hederifolium*, has self-sown and multiplied its tubers into a dense carpet, the pink shuttlecocks jostling one another by the thousand in the autumn. Take a right turn and you find yourself following a path driven through the lower of the main borders, again planted with pastel colours.

There are large clumps here of the ice plant, *Sedum spectabile*; its flat heads of carmine flowers above silvery succulent foliage are visited by multitudes of butterflies. Other clumps are of *Astrantia major*, always intriguing for its starched ruff of bracts which sets off the tuft of slender florets that compose the flower heads. Also here is the pink monkshood, *Aconitum napellus* 'Carneum'.

In the southernmost border are some of Hidcote's most surprising and venturesome plantings: lime-hating rhododendrons, for which special beds of lime-free soil were made up, replacing the alkaline soil that would have been death to such plants.

First, you must go right to the far end to find out what rose is cascading from an ancient yew. It proves to be 'Paul's Himalayan Rambler', set with many thousands of small pink flowers in summer. Just below it runs a stretch of drainage ditch, which eventually becomes a stream. Before it disappears into the conduit its banks are planted with the North American skunk cabbage, *Lysichiton americanus*, which has massive yellow arum flowers in spring and, later, luxuriant paddle-shaped leaves.

From the south border the naturally limey soil was dug out and replaced with a compost of lime-free loam, sawdust and ash from the nearby railway sidings. It promoted

Hesperis matronalis, *Deutzia* × *elegantissima* 'Fasciculata' and *Rosa* 'Felicia' in a dense assembly of summer flowers in the Old Garden.

OPPOSITE Circular staddle stones from old haystacks are used extensively in the paths in the Old Garden.

LEFT The lavender-blue *Rhododendron augustinii* growing successfully in the lime-free border.

a site where it is possible for the rhododendrons and other plants with an aversion to lime to grow happily, such as *Magnolia sieboldii* subsp. *sinensis*, which has single white flowers embellished with a boss of crimson stamens at the heart and a remarkable fruity scent. A specially notable Nepalese species of elephant's ears is *Bergenia ciliata*, with enormous leaves that are covered with a layer of fine hairs, unlike all other bergenias, which have glossy foliage.

The south wall of the Old Garden runs here and it is clothed with wisteria for spring, followed later by the climbing *Hydrangea anomala* subsp. *petiolaris* with ivory lacecap flowers. The rhododendrons are small-flowered types, notably the blue *Rhododendron augustinii*.

Other plants usually seen growing in woodland flourish in the shade here. Among them are the orchid-like *Roscoea cautleoides* with strange yellow flowers and, in a cleft in some rockwork, the tropical-looking *Fascicularia bicolor*, a plant of Chilean origin belonging to the pineapple family that produces blue flowers at the heart of the odd rosette of spiky leaves, which turn scarlet at the base. Less esoteric are the stands of the ordinary Solomon's seal, *Polygonatum* × *hybridum*, and patches of the easy-going creeping *Cotoneaster dammeri*. In a corner where two lengths of the end wall meet at right angles grows the evergreen clinging *Hydrangea serratifolia*, which in summer is massed with ivory flowers. Another of the same family to be found further along is *Pileostegia viburnoides*, evergreen and again one of the very few self-clinging flowering climbers, also ivory in its colouring. The path brings us back to the wrought iron gates separating the Old Garden from the rest of Hidcote, which always stand open, inviting you to leave now this softly coloured area where all has the serenity of the home base and explore the garden's wider horizons of the imagination.

The WHITE GARDEN
and the MAPLE GARDEN

Impatience grips you as you go from the Courtyard through the house and cross the little 'front garden' to meet suddenly your first thrilling sight of the Great Alley. From your viewpoint of the seat at its head it takes a while to recover your breath and reorientate yourself before you are ready to explore the first of the enclosures that adjoin this wondrous triumph of garden scene painting. The first of these is the White Garden.

The dominant theme of the White Garden (3), stated by flowers in partnership with plants with silvery encrustations on leaf and stem, is emphasized by the way all are thrown into sharp relief by the darkness of the enclosing yew hedges and by the deep green of the box in which the topiary and the edgings are carried out. But the White Garden has a secondary theme: it has a network of many curves. You enter the garden through a narrow arch cut in the yew and exit by way of another arch. The improbable topiary birds have absurdly rounded forms and stand on circular bases. The edgings that frame the flower beds are curved to make a broken circle. The steps up to the terrace where the dominating cedar stands have wing walls that rise in prominent humps at the ends. The second motif is another unifying element.

Once this area was a phlox garden, a fashionable garden component in the 1920s, but the plants became infected by the eelworm pest and a grouping of white plants was made to take their place. It is possible that the idea came from Johnston's American novelist friend Edith Wharton, who is believed to have made one of the first white gardens, though the idea is also suggested in Gertrude Jeykll's book *Colour Schemes for the Flower Garden*.

Spring is announced here by the appearance of clumps of tulips of the 'White Triumphator' variety, an old member of the Lily-flowered Group with blooms composed of tapering segments, giving them an elegant appearance.

It is in summer, though, that this garden begins to make its strongest impact, when the white peonies come out. Then the 'Gruss an Aachen' roses are in flower. This is a cluster-flowered rose long preserved in this garden, a child of the famous 'Frau Karl Druschki' but very unlike it in flower, having flattened instead of pointed blooms that

Plants with bold, dramatic foliage such as *Acanthus* (foreground, right) add variety to the mannered planting and the curved topiary in the White Garden.

Close-up of the treasured 'Gruss an Aachen' rose, showing its prolific flowering potential.

are palest pink for a few days but quickly fade to white. Other shrubs here include *Deutzia setchuenensis* var. *corymbiflora*, the finest of its entire genus, and the strange *Fuchsia magellanica* var. *molinae*, brought from Chile by Clarence Elliott, one of Johnston's plantsman friends.

Then, too, the white bells of the *Campanula latifolia* var. *alba* open. This is a most valuable herbaceous plant, since when it has done flowering it leaves behind rosettes of bright green foliage lying close on the ground and persisting through the winter. On the ground that slopes upwards towards the house grows a seashore perennial of unusual boldness in all respects, *Crambe maritima*, once known as a wild plant on sand dunes. In garden soil its leaves become huge, matching the scale of its white inflorescences, which are formed like summer clouds.

There is groundwork here in summer of the daisy-flowered *Anthemis punctata* subsp. *cupaniana*. This is accompanied by *Convolvulus cneorum*, an all-silver shrub of Mediterranean origin. Its flowers are like those of the execrated bindweed, but in spite of the filial association it is faultless.

Through this layer white *Lilium martagon* var. *album*, with its Turk's cap flowers, appears in early summer, followed later by the spires of the Cape hyacinth, *Galtonia candicans*. This South African bulb proves surprisingly hardy where the soil drains sharply, as here, where it has the help of the roots of the topiary and other plants.

For the late summer white petunias are added, together with the perennial but doubtfully hardy *Osteospermum* 'White Pim', another South African which lolls about giving a long succession of elegant white daisies with petals that are blue on the

The White Garden gains strikingly from the passage of the sun, flashes of strong light alternating with shadow.

undersides but revealed only late in the afternoon when the flowers have folded up for the night.

The hedge that divides the White Garden from the Maple Garden is draped in summer with ropes of small scarlet flowers

BELOW *Hydrangea arborescens* subsp. *discolor* 'Sterilis' flowers abundantly in the Maple Garden.

RIGHT The central box-edged beds in the Maple Garden are changed with the seasons. On this occasion they were planted with heliotrope and the feathery-leaved cineraria.

reaching to the tops. These are made in a single season by a trailing plant native to Chile, *Tropaeolum speciosum*. This is a relative of the humble annual nasturtium grown from a packet of seed, but dependably perennial, once the difficulty of establishing it in peaty soil has been overcome. It makes one of Hidcote's spectacular moments.

It helps set the scene of the Maple Garden (4), which takes its name from bushes of ancient lineage that grow here. In contrast to the sobriety of the section of garden we have just left all is richness again here. At once you meet twin box-edged beds where one of the garden's few essays in summer bedding is carried out annually. The plants used may well be one of the varieties – long preserved for its strong scent – of the tender heliotrope, its perfume filling the air round a seat commanding a view through the White Garden and a lower part of the Old Garden.

Two large Italian terracotta pots standing in little exedras in the brick retaining wall also have seasonal occupants. I recall one year admiring a particularly good group made with the shrubby *Abutilon* 'Canary Bird' and the spreading mallow *Malva sylvestris* 'Primley Blue'.

With purplish bronze leaves divided in so complex a fashion that they appear like lace, the maples carry the cumbersome name *Acer palmatum* var. *dissectum* Atropurpureum Group, treasured in Japanese gardens for centuries. Not often is it seen in so contrived an environment as this; usually it has a place in informal woodland gardens. It has a slow-growing partner in the *Magnolia stellata*. This takes its name, of course, from the shape of the white flowers that come out in March, claiming for the bush a sheltered position where they are not carried off prematurely by spring frost.

Just inside this enclosure, which is mostly planted in rich colourings suggested by the purple of the maple, is a mass planting of a cultivar of the hardy *Fuchsia magellanica*, the additional term 'Variegata' applying to the leaves. When they unfold they have a pink tint, half copper, which is joined by grey and green, and during the summer all three colours are subtly interwoven, their intensity changing as each leaf matures. In one corner of this area grows the evergreen Mexican orange *Choisya ternata*. Surprisingly, given that it is of exotic origin, it is hardy enough to suffer no more than scorching of the bright green evergreen leaves in the coldest winters. These leaves prove aromatic when crushed, while the white flowers are sweetly scented, and though they mostly appear in spring they often recur as an autumn crop.

Three hardy perennials are prominent here in summer: *Knautia macedonica*, a crimson scabious; *Veronica gentianoides*, which carries its late spring flowers of sky blue in tall spires, the plant itself making a dense mat of foliage over the surface; and the tall *Macleaya microcarpa*, a 6-foot/1.75-metre plant with spires of fluffy apricot flowers and 'chiselled' grey leaves tinted with copper. Near here the rampant climbing rose 'Paul's Himalayan Musk' soars into an ancient holly tree, embellishing it in early summer with multitudes of scented pink flowers.

Small in area though it is, the White Garden has dramatic large-leaved plants, such as silver-leaved cardoons (foreground, right).

The CIRCLE,
the FUCHSIA GARDEN and
the BATHING POOL GARDEN

The cross axis that begins at the Circle (5) – the second of the series of individual gardens that make up the Great Alley – moves from simplicity to complexity and then back to even more severe simplicity in the *cabinet de verdure* at its southern end.

Most of the year the Circle itself is almost entirely green, but in late spring it is filled with flower and scent, pheasant-eye narcissi opening the season. Then the four quadrants of lilac bushes are in bloom. These are not lilacs of the familiar kind seen

The Circle, with its lilac bushes, is the fulcrum from which four paths and a subsidiary vista radiate. The south path (BELOW) leads into the Fuchsia and Bathing Pool Gardens.

The parterre in the Fuchsia Garden is packed with *Scilla siberica* in spring.

later in the Rose Walk but a hybrid closer to the wild lilac that came originally from Eastern Europe and is known as the Rouen lilac: *Syringa × chinensis*. It gets its common name from its nascence, probably by chance, in the late eighteenth century, in the Botanic Garden at Rouen, but its Latin title is a botanical absurdity, since the parents are the common and the 'Persian' kind, itself an ancient hybrid.

Between these and the circle of brick paving that encloses the fairy ring of turf two hellebores are grown: the white Lenten hellebore, *Helleborus orientalis* subsp. *orientalis*, and the Corsican species, *H. argutifolius* (syn. *H. corsicus*), admired for the sculptural quality of the plant when it is set with jade-green leaves and the large number of bunches of pale greenish yellow flowers.

Several plants join hands to make up groundwork. In parts the soil is covered with the white strawberry-flowered *Potentilla alba* and the white-flowered form of blue-eyed Mary, *Omphalodes verna*. Also taking a place in this assembly is a small-growing species of lady's mantle, *Alchemilla conjuncta*, which has scalloped hairy leaves with a silken lining underneath, turned up at the edges to make a gossamer ring.

While to the north the Circle is bounded by yew hedging, on its south side stands the most celebrated of Hidcote's 'tapestry' hedges, composed of holly, green and copper

beech. The foliage of all three intermingles and changes colour as the season progresses.

Immediately behind the hedge, just inside the Fuchsia Garden (6), to which you are admitted by one of the many inviting openings, thriving in soil that must be tightly interlaced with the hedge's roots, grows what must be one of the most adaptable of the hardy fuchsias, *F. magellanica* 'Thompsonii', which is brighter in the scarlet of its tube and sepals, paler in its purple corolla, than its parent species.

The densely planted box-edged beds of hardy fuchsias have other occupants that put on a dramatic performance in spring. Then, the fuchsias having been cut to the ground, the soil is completely carpeted with a sheet of intense blue from the bulbs of *Scilla siberica* that lie beneath the surface, having seeded themselves year after year. As the scillas' leaves die down the fuchsias grow again, soon taking over completely and filling the beds with dense foliage.

On the wall to the left as you enter – the reverse of the wall round part of the Old Garden – you can see the brackets that once supported overhanging glass panels of the same pattern as those on the south wall in the Courtyard, one of the devices for warding off the effects of winter cold from shrubs of doubtful hardiness. A survivor from the original planting, the large-leaved *Pittosporum dallii*, has shown it needed no such

In summer the *Scilla siberica* in the Fuchsia Garden give way to a display of dwarf fuchsias, which forms part of the vista towards the handsome pediment of the *cabinet de verdure*, clipped in yew.

comfort. One of the New Zealand species, it is now a large round evergreen bush, but, in spite of all its years, yet to produce any of its reputedly perfumed white flowers.

Trained against the wall, *Indigofera amblyantha*, with feathery, almost mimosa-like foliage, puts out sprays of tiny bright pink flowers in late summer. A favourite rose here has long been 'Rose d'Amour', a variety said to have been known to flower in Venice on St Mark's Day, festival of the city's patron saint, on 25 April, and believed to have been the rose favoured as a buttonhole by the Comte d'Orsay, an eighteenth-century French dandy who settled in London, where he won a reputation as an artist. Another is 'Cupid', a mysterious peach-coloured single rose of unknown parentage. In the summer large fuchsia plants are brought out from the greenhouse and planted here.

The four varieties of fuchsias that fill the box-outlined beds have all been chosen for the compact fashion in which they grow. *Fuchsia magellanica* var. *gracilis* 'Variegata' takes the round centre bed. The others are 'Tom Thumb', which is believed to have come originally from France in the middle of the nineteenth century; its paler sport 'Lady Thumb', which arose in Britain more than a hundred years later; and 'Dunrobin Bedder', named for a famous Highland castle garden.

Go down the steps between the pair of topiary peacocks set in a low box hedge, which have preened themselves there since the garden's very earliest days, and you enter the Bathing Pool Garden (7). Spring begins here with the flowering of the blue groundwork of the Caucasian forget-me-not, *Brunnera macrophylla*, and the narrow-leaved lungwort, *Pulmonaria angustifolia* 'Azurea'. Soon the theme is taken up by the spreading evergreen shrub on the left of the steps, *Osmanthus delavayi*, which has perfumed white flowers of tubular shape and, curiously, is related to the olive.

The magnolia near by, *Magnolia* × *soulangeana*, commemorates in its specific name one Etienne Soulange-Bodin, a former cavalry officer who, after the defeat of 1815, took up gardening and crossed magnolias at the Royal Institute of Horticulture which he founded near Paris, producing this, one of the most successful hybrid plants of all time. 'The rising taste for gardening', he wrote in 1819 in a letter to the English *Gardener's Magazine*, 'becomes one of the most agreeable guarantees of the repose of the world.' His own description of his name plant as having 'wide spreading, brilliant flowers in which purest white is tinged with a purplish hue' puts it aptly.

This is quickly followed by *Rhododendron augustinii*, one of the few blue-flowering rhododendron species. This bush honours in its name Augustine Henry, an Irish doctor who, from the time he was stationed in Western China in 1882, studied the flora of the remote regions there for nearly twenty years, during which he sent more than 150,000 specimens to Kew.

Summer brings to these areas the incomparable white cluster-flowered rose Iceberg, a product of the German rose breeder Reimer Kordes and one of the finest ever raised. Underneath it grows *Geranium nodosum*, a determined hardy species which has lilac flowers all through the summer and autumn.

The plantings within the small area south of the pool itself are especially interesting. The spring polyanthus are the pink 'Guinevere'. This is a survivor of the Garryard

Looking back across the Bathing Pool towards the Circle, between the twin topiary peacocks.

The fine old Italian terracotta pots in the Italian House garden are planted with hostas in the Jekyllian style. In the lower right-hand corner is a reproduction of one of the Georgian reeded seats in Lawrence Johnston's collection.

Series, characterized by their bronze leaves and the first of which was found in a garden round a house called Garryard in the west of Ireland. Next comes one of the most spectacular of the blue Tibetan poppies, known as *Meconopsis* × *sheldonii*, a hybrid which carries its Surrey raiser's name. It is followed by the willow gentian, *G. asclepiadea*, with 24-inch/60-centimetre arching stems that each carry a spray of rich blue trumpet flowers. A little later comes *Saxifraga fortunei*, a clump former with scalloped bronze leaves, red beneath, and sprays of white flowers like moths. It carries the name of another plant collector in China, Robert Fortune, who was sent there in 1848 by the East India Company to study the tea-growing industry and introduced plants to Britain from gardens and nurseries, having already made a botanizing trip to the Far East.

Contrasting sharply with these in flower and form is a bugbane, so called for having once been used as an insect deterrent, *Actaea* (syn. *Cimicifuga*) *racemosa*, appealing in its hummocks of fern-like leaves and slim ivory flower spires alike. Meanwhile, at intervals all through the season the retaining wall behind is hung with the white Italian *Corydalis ochroleuca* as well as the wild yellow one.

Inside the adjoining Italian House enclosure all is shaded by tall yew hedges and nearby flowering cherries. The yellow-flowered *Clematis tangutica* subsp. *obtusiuscula* drapes one wall; it has sepals that form lantern-shaped flowers that are followed by 'old man's beard' seedheads. It is thickly underplanted with a specially fine leaf form of *Bergenia cordifolia* and the male fern. Once there were tubs here, planted with tree peonies, but their place is now taken by large terracotta pots with *Rhus typhina*, the stag's horn sumac, a novel use for the gaunt flat-topped bush which exploits its giant, complicated leaves. In the loggia some of the less demanding begonias usually stand about in pots for the summer. Hostas are similarly grown as pot plants in this area.

A timber arch leading to the next enclosure forms a stage for a rare member of the vine family, *Vitis davidii*. This is grown for the splendour of its huge heart-shaped leaves in the autumn, when they take on the crimson of the more familiar *Vitis coignetiae*. The cherries beyond this are the everyday bright pink 'Kanzan' (the name is that of a mountain in China); this was a novelty when it was planted in the 1920s.

While there is a specimen here of the pink North American dogwood *Cornus florida* f. *rubra*, the main woody plant is the tree-like *Hydrangea villosa*. Its long tapering leaves have the texture of velvet and its lacecap flowers are always blue, whatever the acid-alkaline balance of the soil, making it unique in this great family of bushes, which are otherwise blue only on lime-free soil. During their time here these have been cut back hard to regenerate them, but they have grown up readily and now stand tall again, shading the ground beneath them, which has been planted thickly with hostas. Hostas are, of course, noted mainly for foliage that is heavily engraved by the veins, always lush and well poised, but they deserve recognition also for their trumpet flowers arranged in little spires running from white through shades of mauve to a rich purple.

It is the deepest coloured of the whole genus, *Hosta ventricosa*, that is used here, in company with a lesser species, *H. lancifolia*, which is narrow in foliage and makes a specially tight clump. *Helleborus argutifolius* grows here again, seeding itself about and giving a concentrated spring show to the area with its greenish flowers and its splendid foliage. Before you reach the Stream Garden the opening in the hedge is marked by flanking clumps of a curious native plant: this is the butcher's broom, *Ruscus aculeatus*. The leaves of this suckering little bush have been modified to become like spines. The flowers are so small as to be never noticed, but eventually they are succeeded by berries that take on a bright scarlet. It was given its common name because butchers of former times used clusters of its stiff stems tied together to make brushes with which to clean their blocks.

Some of the pots in the Italian House garden are planted for the summer with large-leaved begonias, others permanently with bushes of the stag's horn sumac.

The RED BORDERS

In her influential *Colour Schemes for the Flower Garden*, which first came out in 1914 and was reprinted and republished in several revised editions in her time, and has appeared in further editions since it emerged from copyright, Gertrude Jekyll put forward ideas, plans and planting schemes for several one-colour gardens that have become classic principles of garden making. Blue gardens, yellow gardens, white gardens, pink gardens – she suggested and designed all. This was the most influential of her books, actually her last, and its power has increased rather than diminished. But nowhere in it does she suggest a garden devoted to red flowers. Where, then, if Johnston could not have picked up the idea from Miss Jekyll, the high priestess of the craft of 'painting with plants', was the inspiration for the Red Borders (8) engendered? Here is another of the garden's intriguing imponderables.

Had the question been put to Johnston, it is doubtful that he would have given a direct answer, for he seems to have worked much by inspiration, responding to a sudden surge of the imagination, rather than to any carefully laid or long pondered plan. Given his quiet, retiring disposition, it is surprising that he should have made anything so outrageously daring at the very heart of the garden.

For daring the Red Borders are, perhaps the most daringly conceived and executed of all garden colour schemes. And unlike others this one has rarely been copied or attempted again. Was it, perhaps, an experiment that succeeded? Something that, having satisfied himself with other colour schemes elsewhere in the garden, he thought he might try with a practised hand? That he made paintings of these borders and hung the canvases either side of his bed suggests its accomplishment must have had a very special appeal for him.

Though he added purple-leaved shrubs to the scheme there was no compromising about the ends of the borders. He did not allow them to slip into softer colourings, as Gertrude Jekyll had suggested in her borders.

At the west end he draped over the brickwork the purple-leaved vine, *Vitis vinifera* 'Purpurea'. Seen from the gazebo steps, the borders are bounded by a 'tapestry' hedge in which copper beech contrasts with the green of other species of hedging plants. The red flowers are in fact always seen within the context of woody plants

Full of flowers in summer, the Red Borders are among the most exciting incidents in the whole garden. The flowers are supported by the purple leaves of the background trees.

LEFT
ABOVE Sudden shafts of sunlight give a
radiance to the 'tapestry' hedges and the young
growth of the ornamental grasses which
are part of the Red Borders' composition.
BELOW, LEFT Neatly mown and regularly watered,
the turf preserves an architectural element
in the profusion of flowers and foliage.
BELOW, RIGHT For the summer weeks potted plants
are stood about the garden in the Continental style.

THIS PAGE
ABOVE, LEFT The south pavilion commands
a view of the whole of the Long Walk.
ABOVE, RIGHT The strict formality of the Stilt Garden
is revealed as the visitor follows the Red Border.
RIGHT Tulips make their bold effect in late spring
and purple-leaved cordylines are plunged in the
ground in their pots for the summer.

grown simply for the purple colouring of their foliage. Some of these are small trees; others are grown as shrubs. All benefit from frequent pruning to encourage them to produce the fresh new wood with leaves in which the purple pigment is exhibited at its liveliest.

The boldest foliage effect is made by the 'Crimson King' cultivar of the Norway maple, *Acer platanoides,* a strong-growing tree. More slight are the examples of the purple-leaved plum, *Prunus cerasifera* 'Pissardii' (the cultivar name commemorates a French gardener employed by the Shah of Persia who had noticed it growing). Slighter still is a form of the common wild blackthorn with dainty purple leaves.

Several barberries have a place in the scheme. Here, too, are frequent examples of the culinary sage in its purple form. The purple-leaved New Zealand *Phormium tenax* Purpureum Group has proved hardy enough in this garden, which scarcely favours plants on the borderline of hardiness.

Spring in the red borders opens with many clumps of tulips that are added temporarily each year in foreground bays, and by crown imperials, *Fritillaria imperialis,* with rufous flowers that are said in legend to be for ever obliged to nod in shame because they grew wild along the Via Crucis.

These are quickly followed by the splendid great flowers of the Oriental poppies, followed by the scarlet Jerusalem cross, *Lychnis chalcedonica,* one of the few herbaceous perennials to come to us from Russia and one of the few we have with no

Fuchsias of the triflora type, with elongated tubes, are prominent among the plants brought out from the greenhouses for the summer (LEFT) and contribute to the Red Borders' display (RIGHT).

trace of any other tint in its colouring. With these flower some of the hybrid herbaceous cinquefoils, notably the *Potentilla* 'Gibson's Scarlet', a group much favoured in gardens in the twentieth century.

High summer brings the great flush of colour that has made these borders so famous; it is then that their daring is seen at its most adventurous. The herbaceous plants at their best include that invasive day lily with double orange flowers *Hemerocallis fulva* 'Green Kwanso' (syn. 'Kwanso Flore Pleno'), imported from Japan in the nineteenth century and here allowed to grow as it will. One of its special virtues is that the flowers last considerably longer than those of other day lilies.

Flowering continuously week after summer week some of the cluster-flowered roses have a place in the scheme. Dahlias are added plentifully for late summer, notably the old variety 'Bishop of Llandaff,' so fashionable today but preserved for many decades at Hidcote for the sake of its bronze foliage and the orange flowers that fit so well into this colour scheme.

Though not dependably hardy, some of the tall-growing lobelias of the *cardinalis* type have long been cultivated here, adding spires of large red flowers, so different from the familiar bedding lobelia. The exotic-looking cannas with bronze and purple leaves and red and orange flowers are added annually, as is the flat-growing scarlet verbena named after Lawrence Johnston. Bronze-leaved cordylines are sunk temporarily in the ground in their pots. During the summer season purple delphiniums grow here and in autumn their stately poise is repeated by a form of a late monkshood, *Aconitum carmichaelii*.

OPPOSITE 'Architectural' plants like this foreground purple-leaved cordyline contrast sharply with the roses and hardy perennials in the Red Borders.

ABOVE, LEFT The old 'Bishop of Llandaff' dahlia has long been cherished at Hidcote.

ABOVE, RIGHT The double *Hemerocallis fulva* 'Green Kwanso' and *Lobelia* × *speciosa* 'Cherry Ripe'.

The WINTER BORDER *and* *the* ALPINE TERRACE

If instead of exploring in detail the Red Borders you turn left just west of the Circle, you quickly come to a long and broad path that leads past the Winter Border and along the bottom of the Long Walk towards Hidcote's Alpine Terrace.

The Winter Border (9) has to take its name from the bushes of *Sarcococca* which have suckered prodigally. The white flowers, stained lightly with pink, come out in winter – not spectacularly like those of the witch hazels and the mahonias (of which there is one example here), but they make their mark with their powerful perfume, often likened to the cloying scent of privet on a summer's day.

A *Photinia* bush stands on the corner; its leaves open red, changing later to give it a green and highly polished livery. Then comes a fine magnolia tree of the rich pink-flowered series of Cornish fame, *Magnolia campbellii* subsp. *mollicomata*, a hostage to fortune since its magnificence in blossom is always likely to be shattered in a night in March by a cruel frost. Still, gardeners of over-powering enthusiasm like Lawrence Johnston are always ready to take this risk, even though they may see it flower only occasionally and then but for a few days.

Seldom molested by harsh weather is a splendid tulip species that comes out in late spring. It is *Tulipa sprengeri* and its flowers are a coppery shade, elegantly poised on 24-inch/60-centimetre stems.

A massive bush of the southern European *Viburnum tinus* has been trained and clipped into a great box-like piece of topiary. It nearly conceals the south gazebo, which is approached by a flight of steps with risers hidden by neatly clipped *Cotoneaster horizontalis*, smothered with scarlet berries in autumn, and, in this position, shunned by the birds. On the lowest step, chained against theft, are two very old watering cans, said to be of a pattern used at Versailles in its prime. If they were, one must feel sorry for whoever had to handle them, for even empty they are surely the heaviest and most difficult of watering cans to manipulate.

Planted to enjoy the shelter of the west face of the south gazebo but allowed to express the natural willowiness of its lax branches is a 'tree' of the Moroccan broom,

The winter border lies just south of the Red Border on a lower level. A mahonia has been allowed to spread into a thicket here.

Cytisus battandieri. The large heads of yellow flowers are strongly scented of pineapple.

Now we have reached the Alpine Terrace (10), one of Hidcote's most original innovations. Ever sensitive to horticultural fashion but ready to adapt it to his own purposes, quite late in the garden's development Johnston took up seriously alpine plant cultivation, which was the rage in the 1920s, stimulated by the books of the plant collector Reginald Farrer, one the most eloquent and spirited of garden writers with a most persuasive pen.

Home to many 'rock plants', the Alpine Terrace is always said to resemble no other rock garden. The principal purpose in its construction was to provide efficient drainage of the soil to prevent moisture lodging about the plants' roots in winter and also to prevent harm coming to the top growth during our rainy winters. In their natural home many of the plants most desired by those who attempt to bring them into cultivation lie under a thick coverlet of snow, with an icy crust on top, for months at a stretch. They do not take kindly to the alternations of damp and cold which they receive on rock gardens in our climate. To save them from harm under these circumstances many rock garden enthusiasts prop panes of glass over their most treasured plants for the winter months. With his uncontrollable zeal Johnston did many times better than this.

Not only did he eschew the whole idea of attempting to replicate a fragment of

Tasmanian tree ferns, a pre-war feature of the Fern Dell, have been replanted in recent years and so far have prospered. They are wrapped up against winter cold. The hydrangea flowering on the right is *H. aspera* subsp. *sargentiana*.

alpine scenery but he decided to grow his collection of such plants in two terraces, formal in character, one a couple of feet above the level of the path, the second behind it another couple of feet higher. The drainage was excellent. Then he went further. He had sockets sunk into the ground into which posts were inserted for the winter. These provided the supports for a timber framework on which for the dangerous months were placed a series of glass lights to make the perfect shelter for plants of this nature. In summer the whole structure could easily be dismantled and stored away.

Of course, during the lean years the equipment went out of use, but it has now been replicated and the two tiers have been replanted with a huge collection of alpine plants, many of which will have nothing but this special treatment. The number of different species recorded in the inventory reaches nearly a hundred, including many rare bulbs which are often some of the most difficult to get to live to flower another day.

The silvery saxifrages that thrust out long sprays of flowers are set in crevices in the walls. So are the Californian lewisias, which have fleshy starfish-like clusters of foliage and sprays of enchanting copper, red or pink flowers. There are miniature members of the South American bromeliad or pineapple family. There are grey-leaved New Zealand celmisias, some of the most difficult scions of the vast daisy family. There are spreading carpets of the flat-growing phlox from the Rockies. There are tiny daphne bushes that otherwise almost defy cultivation. There are succulent daisies of South African origin. There are enchanting miniature irises. There are low-growing New Zealand leptospermums. There are even succulent plants usually grown in greenhouses – aloes, fleshy-leaved stonecrops and even, in a specially sheltered corner, a prickly pear.

This is an area of the garden where one can readily regret the Hidcote policy of not putting labels on plants, decided upon so that the garden should retain its character as one man's – a plantaholic's and garden zealot's – private paradise which it is a privilege for us to enter and enjoy.

On the south side there is an area known as the fernery, or fern corner, where, unpretentious but deserving special comment, several of Hidcote's most dramatic plants flourish. The three tree ferns Johnston planted here are further testimony of his catholic taste in plants. The originals were long since lost but have now been replaced with examples of *Dicksonia antarctica*. Their 6-foot/1.75-metre trunks indicate that they must have begun life in his time – perhaps before, so slow is this tree to develop.

It builds its height by only the shallow depth of the fronds' bases, made afresh each year. These fronds are like giant versions of those of our native male fern but can reach out to 6 feet/1.75 metres in length. This species is one of the tree ferns that grow wild in Australia, most notably in Tasmania, where there are forests almost exclusive to it; some plants are culled for the timber and for the European plant trade under a protected plant scheme. The plant's name commemorates an otherwise forgotten English botanist of the eighteenth century and the early nineteenth, one James Dickson (1738–1822).

Strangely, it can be propagated by setting pieces of the trunk, even poor aged ones, in light soil, as 'massive cuttings'. They root almost with the readiness of willow wands or the trunks of the mulberry tree. Legend has it that some of the ancient tree ferns admired in Cornish gardens were grown from logs put on show at the Great Exhibition of 1851 and taken down there when the show was dismantled.

A second plant of special interest here is the large-growing tree peony named *Paeonia rockii*. The specific name honours an American botanist, traveller and student of the Orient, Joseph Rock, who collected plants in western China and Tibet in the 1930s. His eponymous tree peony, a rare plant in cultivation and in the wild, has saucer-sized white flowers heavily blotched with maroon at the centre, where they frame a central boss of golden-tipped stamens. In flower it is one of the most impressive plants of its entire large family. Such is its exclusiveness that, unlike Mr Dickson's tree fern, it often defies those who attempt to propagate it by way of cuttings.

Other ferns at home here include the remarkable Chilean species *Blechnum chilense*, with lengthy ladder-like fronds that persist through our winters. In moist soil it becomes a fern of striking handsomeness when it spreads wildly, as it will after a few seasons.

The time for dismantling the covering structure which protects the more vulnerable plants in the Alpine Terrace comes with the spring. It will be replaced in autumn.

MRS WINTHROP'S GARDEN

Dedicated by name to Lawrence Johnston's mother, Mrs Winthrop's Garden (11), the small section of Hidcote Manor Garden deeply enclosed by sheltering 'tapestry' hedges of green and copper beech and lime, is another startling surprise.

But did she ever sit there on a summer's day? Her designer son did not provide her with much comfort, for he placed his collection of Georgian garden seats not inside it but outside, looking away across to the southernmost extremity. True, the brick tiers with which its architecture is defined and the slope thus exploited are known to have been strewn with blue and gold cushions on fine days. This meant she would have had to recline in Arab fashion, should she so wish – not very dignified for a lady of the Manor, an American heiress brought up in exquisite comfort with servants to minister to her every whim. Another of the Hidcote puzzles! The colour scheme here is blue and yellow. Was this her favourite colour pairing? Or a wish unfulfilled in her person, for if she was ever photographed she was usually seen wearing sombre grey.

Standing in the centre of Mrs Winthrop's Garden is a sundial. The stone plinth bears the inscription '1799 Kew Bridge 1899', hinting at a sell-off of relics of the bridge when it was rebuilt. In the brick arcs are plinths to take tall plants of the shrubby verbena *Aloysia triphylla*, returned to the greenhouses for winter protection, and, by long-established tradition, mature plants of the spiky *Agave americana* also stood out here for the summer.

The yellow and blue display in Mrs Winthrop's Garden is at its height in early summer, but as the season advances much tidying is carried out to leave the area clear for a successive burst of the same colourings.

In Mrs Winthrop's Garden spiky-leaved variegated yuccas and agaves are added in pots during the summer.

The ground-covering and herbaceous plants vary from carpets of homely cottage garden species like the yellow-leaved creeping Jenny, *Lysimachia nummularia* 'Aurea', the blue-flowered Hidcote comfrey and borage, large-leaved *Brunnera* and silvery *Stachys*, and the favourite old lady's mantle, *Alchemilla mollis*, to lordly delphiniums and intricately leaved monkshoods, aconitums, aquilegias and campanulas. To emphasize the yellow component a marguerite, *Argyranthemum* 'Jamaica Primrose', is added for the summer, while the distinctive Hidcote hypericum shrub has its place here, as does the yellow-leaved form of the hedging plant *Lonicera nitida* called 'Baggesen's Gold'.

The intricate foliage of *Melianthus major* adds a contrasting 'architectural' touch here.

The LONG WALK, *the* THEATRE LAWN *and the* STILT GARDEN

Retracing your footsteps back to the Great Alley and by way of the steps leading up from the Red Borders takes you up to the level of the Stilt Garden, from which you can glimpse the distant prospect of cloud and sky from a magnificent wrought iron gate – 'heavenwards', as visitors often say.

Marking the transition between levels are elegant twin gazebos, sometimes styled the pavilions. They are built in brick but have steep ogival roofs tiled with stone and each capped with a ball finial. Inside, the ceilings are frescoed, by Johnston's hand, it is always claimed, the north one depicting Chinese urns. The walls are part lined with old Delft tiles. While some, most likely Dutch, show country scenes, others form a composite picture of a ship in full sail. Another group depicts a vase of flowers in the Portuguese fashion.

Poised high above the Winter Border, and containing a slate plaque commemorating Lawrence Johnston's genius in creating the garden, the south gazebo is in essence a porch with double doors on two sides. It commands a view of the Long Walk (12), again leading to a gated opening that seems to reveal infinity beyond.

It is a thrilling moment for the first-time Hidcote visitor to stand here and look out along the Long Walk. The surprise at coming across something so different from everything you have seen so far in the garden is overwhelming. French in character, it must surely derive from Johnston's experience of gardens he visited during his stays in France from an early age. Again it benefits from a rise in the natural terrain, and though it is terminated by a fine gateway, from the viewpoint of the south gazebo it seems that it is the sky on which this great avenue is focused.

As with all such allées in France, the Long Walk is defined by tall, immaculately trimmed hedges of hornbeam with loose boskage behind, which enhances the perspective and, by illusion, lengthens the avenue beyond its true size.

But before we explore it let us turn off towards the north for a moment and answer the visitor's question 'Doesn't Hidcote have a lawn?'. Yes, it certainly does: a lawn of something around an acre in extent. But this lawn is in a frame of its own and seems unrelated, in geography and style, to the rest of the garden. For it is

The trunks of the hornbeam trees in the Stilt Garden combine with the walls beside the steps and the hedges to suggest the wings of a stage set in each view of the Great Alley.

Like all of Hidcote's main vistas, the hornbeam-lined Long Walk is focused on a glimpse of the sky – 'heavenwards', some visitors say of this device.

...walls of deep glistening ...blackish on days when the light level is low. The Theatre Lawn (13), as it is known, is another of Hidcote's powerful surprises. You come upon it suddenly as you follow one of the lesser paths or enter by way of a narrow opening in the hedge just past the north gazebo.

The lawn is levelled to something like bowling green standards, in itself an achievement in a garden where the original site was undulating. Doubtless it was created on the 'cut and fill' principle. Using today's earth-moving equipment the task would now be a relatively easy realignment of the natural territory. But back in the early 1920s, when the lawn was made, levelling would have been a formidable undertaking, carried out entirely by hand, the soil being moved either by wheelbarrow or in a two-wheeled farm cart filled by hand shovel and pulled by a patient horse. The final levelling would have been done with a horse-drawn harrow and preparing the surface for sowing on a fine tilth done by the same laborious method.

Speculation has suggested that the Theatre Lawn was created for games to be played there, but the founder's sporting interest was in tennis, for which he had a court made close to the Plant House. At the east end of the lawn were some of the mature trees standing on the site when Johnston arrived, but eventually old age took them over and they had to be felled. They were replaced with the smaller growing hornbeams.

At the opposite end was another clump of beeches, which also had to be felled and replaced, this time with young beech trees. They are partly encircled by a raised terrace, a kind of stage and another echo of a historic convention – many classical designs included an outdoor theatre. The way up to this dais, which has been nicknamed the Bandstand, is by a flight of broad steps with handsome stone finials carved as baskets of fruit set on each of the returns. From time to time plays are performed here: the actors come and go from entrances in the yew hedges and the lawn itself serves as a great auditorium. In autumn the turf covering the dais is spangled with the lilac blooms of autumn crocuses, which have spread in their thousands by the natural process of seeding and corm multiplication.

A break in the lawn's northern stretch of yew hedging reveals a broad north-facing avenue of beech trees backed by an artificially created stretch of woodland. This Beech Alley links the garden with flat landscape to the north across the Vale of Avon. From the great lawn, however, the avenue frames the sky, as other viewpoints of the garden do, rather than framing an eyecatcher. Only when you walk to and reach the gates at the end do you catch a glimpse of that splendid disappearing landscape. The avenue is sealed from the garden by another pair of timber gates like those linking the Courtyard from the Garden Yard, apparently copied from those at nearby Cleeve Priory, illustrated in Gertrude Jekyll's book *Gardens for Small Country Houses*. Again the avenue is one of Hidcote's many surprises, a feature totally unsuspected by the first-time visitor making the tour of this richly embroidered garden. With...

simplicity and sense of repose it helps, as the Theatre Lawn itself does, emphasize the intricacy of the garden's highly imaginative overall architecture.

But we must return yet again to the Great Alley. In the technical vocabulary of garden making the Stilt Garden (14) forms a *palissade à l'Italienne*. The fact that the French is used for the term indicates the main country of adoption of the convention

RIGHT A dais makes a stage at the far end of the Theatre Lawn, with entrances and exits in the surrounding yew hedging for the players to come and go.

BELOW Elderly bushes of tree peonies, hybrids from *Paeonia delavayi*, have flourished for many years at the east end of the Theatre Lawn.

ABOVE The view back towards the house, looking east along the Great Alley from the westernmost end.

CENTRE Looking towards the gateway at the western end of the Great Alley, which gives on to a platform offering a distant prospect towards the Malvern Hills.

of training trees in regular fashion to leave the trunks clean, like stilts, so as to give a formal outline and an area of shade underneath. It can be seen used in the main square or boulevard of every French town and village. Equally, though, the Hidcote hornbeams could claim English descent and be termed 'pleached'. More basically, the Hidcote hornbeams have been described with admirable simplicity as 'empty boxes'.

The panel of grass running westwards beneath the hornbeam stilts is of more exotic and ancient lineage. It follows the shape of pools with a crescent at each end that has been used in gardens for centuries.

The enclosed twin flower beds beyond the hornbeams make the final incident in the long sequence with which the garden's main vista is composed. Surprisingly for low hedges, the enclosing plant is yew, clipped severely. The parallel lines add yet a further touch to the sense of distance achieved. It is the final moment before the great gate piers, topped with their *putti*, frame the western sky.

Surprisingly, also, in so small an area, the four seasons are catered for in the plantings. For winter there is the winter sweet, *Chimonanthus praecox*, admired wherever it is seen for its curious pale yellow flowers, crimson at the heart and heavily perfumed, and the everyday scentless jasmine, *J. nudiflorum*. Both are trained against the arc-shaped wall which seals off the garden environment beyond here and enhances the view between holm oaks and English oaks, across fields and towards the distant hills.

The chief summer display here has been made with yellow mulleins. But the discovery of old photographs has revealed that in Johnston's day the beds were filled with blue anchusas, and an attempt is being made to replicate this.

Several grasses making an effect in late summer find a place here, notably the South American pampas *Cortaderia selloana* 'Sunningdale Silver'. The other main grass is the striped form of the Chinese zebra grass, *Miscanthus sinensis* 'Zebrinus', grown mainly for its barred leaves. These reach their most significant stage in autumm. Then the yew is swagged with an ornamental vine, the large-leaved *Vitis coignetiae*. Of Far Eastern origin, this in autumn takes on claret colourings that brighten before winter cold severs them from their stems.

The most dramatic plant in these beds is a tree deprived of its natural potential by being stooled every spring to force it into making a fresh crop of vigorous whippy stems, each bearing massive heart-shaped leaves. This is the famous foxglove tree, *Paulownia tomentosa*, in this role made to become something like a giant spot-plant incident in a summer bedding scene.

The uninterrupted view from the hilltop platform is made possible by a concealed ha-ha which prevents the grazing sheep and cattle from entering the garden.

Nowhere else in the garden is Hidcote's first principle – of combining architecture carried out in living materials with planting for colour effects that follow one another in a long sequence yet give a plenitude of flowers at any one time – stated more directly than in the Pillar Garden (15). If it had no flowers at all this little area would still be one of great significance and individuality. When seen in uncaptioned photographs it is unmistakably Hidcote.

While the edgings are boldest here and strongly emphasize the geometry, the characterizing effect of the Pillar Garden is the result of a series of identical columns of yew, twenty-two of them all the same – unusual in a topiary garden. Each is fashioned like a great votive candle standing in a massive square sconce. In a formal pattern paths cross one another as a grid. A slight change of level is emphasized by terracing and put to good practical purpose. At the heart lies a panel of turf, across which the slim shadows of the pillars move with the hours.

What inspired it? What can have persuaded this man to have planted so many pieces of identical topiary in so small an area? It is a teasing conundrum that invites speculation. Perhaps Johnston came across the whole collection of clipped yews in a nursery (probably imported from Belgium), liked the look of them all together and bought them up as a job lot. Perhaps, though – a more pleasing theory to play with – the echoes of the Dutch style suggest that he had seen the picture of Rubens's garden at Antwerp. Or he may have known it from a reproduction and his imagination was struck by no more than that. The Pillar Garden is certainly one of the most stylish topiary gardens in the country; others are either a random mixture of shapes or an assortment of figures belonging to one theme, such as the chessmen at Hever Castle in Kent or the fox and hounds that chase one another along the top of one of the yew hedges at Knightshayes in Devon. And, like Mrs Winthrop's Garden, it gains from being so artfully hidden.

Hidcote's Pillar Garden reveals its characterizing element even more resolutely than anywhere else in the garden where a plant is repeated. A mere handful of plants are set out with a bold hand and, taking the stage one by one, provide a series of

Both tree peonies and the herbaceous type are prominent in the borders in the Pillar Garden and have flourished here for decades. Each yew pillar is like a great votive candle standing in a massive square sconce.

themes in this area – daffodils in early spring, alpine campanulas in late spring, followed in flower by tree peonies and then herbaceous peonies, hardy geraniums taking up the relay, mock orange bushes in early summer succeeded by lavender, then fuchsias as summer turns to autumn.

Once the daffodil *Narcissus × johnstonii* 'Queen of Spain' – one of the early hybrids from *N. triandrus* – grew here and played a part in opening the spring show, though it was not named after Lawrence Johnston. However, it did not prove hardy enough and dwindled. Now it is limited here to a mere clump of bulbs. Tulips are planted lavishly in this area, succeeding the up-to-date varieties of daffodils.

Spring is also marked by the blossoming of the pillar-like Japanese cherry 'Amanogawa', planted repeatedly in the lower beds. Translated, the varietal name means 'Celestial River', the Japanese term for what we call the Milky Way. For the spring there are also ground-covering patches of the narrow-leaved blue-flowered lungwort *Pulmonaria angustifolia* 'Azurea'.

The top border, its path fringed with the 'Hidcote' lavender, is devoted largely to white-flowered plants. Enduring architectural form is provided by the dense old plants of *Yucca flaccida*. Defying the saying that this Mexican native flowers only once in a hundred years, in this well-drained situation the Hidcote plant flowers in most summers,

OPPOSITE *Paeonia × lemoinei* 'L'Espérance' – brief in flower but a splendid sight in its glory days.
LEFT, ABOVE A rare sighting of a peony of the herbaceous type: *Paeonia obovata*.
LEFT, BELOW *Paeonia × lemoinei* 'Mme Louis Henry', a tree species of great age.

the rosette of leaves dying with the flower stem but leaving new rosettes to continue the succession.

In early summer repeated bushes of the mock orange *Philadelphus* 'Belle Etoile' bloom here. Each perfumed star-shaped flower of this compact-growing bush is stained with carmine at the heart. Only a little later the hybrid Californian tree poppy *Romneya* × *hybrida* – named in honour of John Thomas Romney Robinson (1792–1882), an Irish astronomer, by a friend who was the botanist first to describe it after its arrival from California – opens its huge papery white flowers, each setting off a massive boss of tightly packed golden stamens. The prolific fashion in which it suckers here shows a liking for soil impoverished by the penetrating roots of the hornbeam hedge behind.

Contemporaneous with this are the flowers of the white fraxinella, *Dictamnus albus*, which will flare briefly if a match is put to the stems. At intervals come the always 'freshly laundered' flowers of the white musk mallow, *Malva moschata* f. *alba*, a native plant whose self-sown seedlings are never unwelcome.

When autumn arrives it is time for the suckering stems of *Physostegia virginiana* to produce their flowers. The common name of 'obedient plant' refers to the way in which the flowers stay in any position where they are pushed on the stem.

Even on a winter's day the Pillar Garden makes a strong impact, the yews having been neatly clipped in the early autumn.

The top path of the Pillar Garden edged with the violet 'Hidcote' lavender, preceded in flower by this bank of *Philadelphus* 'Belle Etoile' (of the Purpureo-maculatus Group).

It is here that the main plantings of the celebrated 'Hidcote' lavender grow, this compact variety with violet flowers making a dramatic edging either side of the path when it is in flower in August. The garden is often given the credit for having raised this remarkable form, as it is believed to be, of the wild Mediterranean lavender, *Lavandula angustifolia*. However, a friend of Johnston's who travelled with him on several plant-collecting trips in Europe told me that south of the Pyrenees they found plenty of lavender of this habit and colouring and he believed that Johnston selected it from collections made there.

Immediately south of the lavender-lined path is a terraced border. Its most striking occupants are the tree peonies, ancient and multi-stemmed. The massive flower heads are stuffed with petals, yellow in some cases and others mottled like blood oranges. These are succeeded in flower by old bushes of a lavender known as 'Hidcote Giant'. Its colouring is a violet tone similar to that of the dwarf 'Hidcote' itself but the plants are altogether more robust and deserve their name. After one has seen large-growing lavenders in the public gardens in Johnston's other home region in the south of France, one is tempted to suspect the same source. In later

Hardy fuchsias have grown to considerable age in several parts of the garden, benefiting from the efficient natural drainage of the soil.

summer the flower relay is taken up by hardy fuchsias making wands 36 inches/90 centimetres tall, interspersed occasionally with the lilac spires of the aromatic Russian sage, *Perovskia*.

Below this the bed is edged with a ribbon of an early-flowering creeping *Campanula* set with thousands of tiny blue bells in late spring, just before the herbaceous peonies open, to be followed in late summer by the flowering of hardy *Agapanthus*. More peonies line the paths running southwards in the grid, but one is lined with the splendid hardy geranium 'Johnson's Blue', a lucky chance seedling sent from Holland and grown from seeds sent there from England. It is named after one of the gardening luminaries of Johnston's day, A.T. Johnson, who wrote eloquently about his abundantly planted woodland and mill gardens in North Wales. The day of both the geranium and peony edgings may be brief but they add to the garden the excitement of keen anticipation to be sure of catching their moments of glory.

As late summer gives way to intimations of autumn the Pillar Garden is overhung by the spicy scent of many plants of *Phlox paniculata*. They are accompanied in sunny seasons by the flowering by a galaxy of bushes of the hardy *Hibiscus syriacus*. Still the succession keeps up, now with the Japanese anemones allowed to have their way of spreading wildly. In winter they helpfully die right away to allow a clear field

for the many bulbs grown here to be seen at their best unhindered by the foliage of other plants.

The east border of the Pillar Garden has a characteristic touch in being the site of a collection of shrub roses of the repeat-flowering Bourbon type. These are direct descendants of the first of the roses that have it in them to flower beyond the June floraison – unlike most of those to be found in Hidcote's Rose Walk, where the garden's old rose collection is preserved. The original natural cross which introduced the repeat-flowering element was one of the most fortunate of plant marriages.

In the Pillar Garden also is a collection of clematis that flower in summer and autumn. They are trained not against trellis as these plants so frequently are but on stout posts set in the ground. When the plants are in leaf and in flower these become pillars of exciting vegetation supporting the area's title. They demonstrate a valuable method of accommodating many varieties within a limited area.

As summer just passes its climax, herbaceous phlox flower freely in the Pillar Garden border, filling the air with a spicy fragrance.

The BULB SLOPE and the STREAM GARDEN

Go to the very top of the Great Alley, pass through the splendid gateway and you stand on an open area of grassland known as the Bulb Slope (or Spring Slope) (16), so called after the bulbs planted in the turf to multiply in their own time and way. Go to the edge of the ha-ha dividing garden from parkland beyond, where cattle graze, and you stand before an inspiring panorama bounded in the far distance by the blue line of the Malvern Hills.

Maple trees take on their rich leaf colouring in autumn in the Bulb Slope, which descends to (BELOW) a lightly shaded area where Lenten hellebores seed themselves with abandon.

LEFT, TOP Daffodils that have naturalized richly in the upper levels of the Stream Garden make a brilliant scene in spring.

LEFT, BOTTOM Leucojums (snowflakes) have also developed large clumps, while epimediums and hostas will carpet the ground when their new foliage develops.

ABOVE The stream has cleft the ground deeply where the descent is greatest, but the necessary bridge commands a fine view across the damp soil plantings.

RIGHT The skunk cabbage, *Lysichiton americanus*, is permanent among these plantings, growing in mud.

In the company of self-sown male ferns, the 'Hidcote Blue' cultivar of *Symphytum*, better known as comfrey.

Just behind you is the hump, of ancient barrow-like shape, that cuts off the Pillar Garden, most likely created from the spoil from levelling. Once this was a traditional rock garden with low-growing shrubs and ample soil pockets for the other plantings. In the Hidcote tradition of always adding more and more garden, a new section of rock garden has now been created here, as a kind of centenary celebration (2007), with help from the custodians of the great rock garden at the Royal Botanic Garden Edinburgh. Open to wind and full sunlight, the site is perfect for such a horticultural endeavour.

Go on further down the slope, making your way between shrubs carpeted by a thick underlayer of periwinkle, and eventually at the lowest point you meet the stream that enters the garden at the highest point in the Old Garden. By the time it has reached this far it has broadened and driven a small ravine, giving the area the name of the Stream Garden (17). By the bridge that spans it is a stand of tall *Cercidiphyllum* trees. In autumn the fallen leaves carpet the ground deeply and have the aroma of strawberry jam being made. Close by is Hidcote's sole supposed 'champion tree', the oriental chestnut *Aesculus indica*, a noble specimen and perhaps the largest of its kind in the land. A viewpoint offers another parkland and farmed panorama across the ha-ha, surmounted in the distance by the tower on Broadway Hill.

Leave this scene and take the path up towards the garden proper, past many trees and shrubs that enjoy the well-watered land here, notably stewartias, rhododendrons, hydrangeas, magnolias and camellias. Herbaceous plants also enjoy the artificially created woodland soil, in particular the hostas, brunneras, the umbrella plant or large-leaved darmera, many hardy geraniums and ferns, all in a richly assorted assembly punctuated at intervals by lilies. Eventually you reach the little packhorse bridge crossing the stream where it intercepts the Long Walk.

ABOVE, LEFT A specially successful flowering ground-coverer in the Stream Garden is the blue *Brunnera macrophylla*, which has spread a weed-excluding carpet over a wide area.

ABOVE, RIGHT The return from the upper regions of the Stream Garden to the Bathing Pool Garden.

Having left the Stream Garden and followed the Long Walk a little way, you come to an inviting opening in the hedge on the left, where both the mood and historical context change abruptly. Curiosity must be satisfied. On entering, at once you are in yet another different style of garden.

The heavily planted Wilderness (18), to the east of the Long Walk, was conceived quite late in the garden's history. Formerly it was called Westonbirt after the great arboretum of that name in the south of Gloucestershire, one of Britain's most spectacular autumn colour gardens. It belongs to the era of the woodland garden, engendered by the great numbers of hitherto unknown, even unsuspected, shrubs that were being sent to Britain from expeditions sponsored by the wealthy and deeply committed amateurs of the early part of the twentieth century, of whom Lawrence Johnston was one. The last area to be planted before the Second World War began, it brought to an end the development of the garden in Johnston's hands and takes the garden to the southernmost escarpment.

This is an area where grass walks wind between plantations of shrubs overhung by an upper layer made by trees. In contrast to other parts of the garden it is shady and verdant. Other such gardens had been made in existing woodlands; Johnston made his own, planting it with his choice of exotic trees, most of them picked out for the hectic colouring their leaves take on before they fall in autumn. Expanding his horticultural horizons beyond the enclosures deriving from much earlier models and his French-inspired tree- or hedge-lined vistas, Johnston became part of this movement with his characteristic enthusiasm and connoisseurship, planting his woodland only with trees most highly prized by this school of gardening. An underplanting of shrubs with leaves that also assume rich colourings of crimson, pink, copper and gold add to this autumn colour pageant.

Gradually the shrubs grew into dense thickets and after thirty years they had become unkempt and began to decline. It was time to clear the entire area of its groundwork and, leaving the trees to prosper, to replant the beds that, by their configuration, made the network of glades. The opportunity was taken to lengthen the season of effect, bringing it forward into the summer. The trees alone were then large enough to put on the exhilarating scene, especially the Japanese maples which had

Although the Wilderness is a network of glades it has one main vista – again towards the sky.

been planted as mere bushes but had by now taken on tree status.

Perpetually shaded by the overhanging canopy of leafy branches, woodland gardens can sometimes be sombre places, especially when there is no sun to peer through, glance on the leaves, throw up the colour of the bark and make dancing patterns of light and dark on the turf. This one is saved from this defect by the ever-present view of openness in the distance as the ground rises to the crest of the hill. Also, in the far distance the silvered stems of the plantation of birch trees poised on the horizon give lightness to the scene. Colchicums planted between them have grown into dense clumps, flowering in autumn.

The first trees you meet after entering the Wilderness from the gap in the hornbeam hedge are three maples, specimens of a variety of oriental origin, *Acer grosseri* var. *hersii*, a sure autumn-colourer but grown principally for the rich cinnamon colouring of its smooth bark, polished in this case by the constant strokings of visitors fascinated by its texture.

Other trees include several species of *Sorbus*; those maples grown for their striped bark but with leaves that take on hectic autumn colourings, notably *Acer pensylvanicum*; a liquidambar, scarcely matched in autumn; and the southern beech, *Nothofagus antarctica*.

LEFT Several of the overhanging Wilderness trees have been planted at the fringe of the bed so that the bark can be enjoyed.

RIGHT The wilderness has a dense underplanting of shrubs which, like the ground-covering plants in other parts of the garden, deny weeds a chance of flourishing.

The shrubby underplanting includes many Lacecap hydrangeas and viburnums, but special mention has to be made of two plants of great rarity, even bafflement. First is the Chilean bamboo *Chusquea culeou*, which has olive-green canes set with leafy clusters all the way along them. The second great curiosity is a tree, *Emmenopterys henryi*, brought from China as long ago as 1907 but planted in very few gardens. Rarely has it flowered anywhere in cultivation yet. It was eighty years after its introduction that it first flowered in Britain. It proved a spectacular sight, with huge bunches of white blooms. Hidcote's tree is still (in 2007) keeping everyone waiting.

Throughout the Wilderness the ground is curiously ridged. This is a relic of the medieval method of 'ridge and furrow' cultivation.

OPPOSITE AND ABOVE In the autumn the leaves of many kinds of trees and shrubs display brilliant colourings, varying from crimson through shades of red and copper to gold.

The PLANT HOUSE

The woodland gardens on which the interests of the luminaries of the horticultural world – whose society Lawrence Johnston enjoyed, if at something of a remove – were concentrated in Hidcote's glory days were populated by magnolias of rare and wonderful vintage and, most prominently, rhododendrons. These they hybridized to produce an increasing range of colourings, often tints of the red that came to be known as cinnabar.

In his characteristically distant way Johnston joined this movement while preserving his originality. For this band of his contemporaries, who gardened on multi-acre estates, herbaceous plants were of little account. Much less were they interested in raising summer flowers from seed or cuttings. Johnston, however, was primarily an artist: all flowers were the colours in his palette and the plants' shapes seemed drawn by his brush. Indeed, year by year his passion to explore and exploit the whole range of garden plants grew ungovernably and as the limitations of his space out of doors narrowed he moved inside. Already he had greenhouses but eventually he built himself a huge plant shelter in order to house an indoor garden.

Neither conservatory nor orangery, the Plant House (19) was nevertheless conceived as part of the overall decorative fancy, hardly like any other plant house. Facing south and sited on the edge of the disguised and plant-decorated kitchen garden, it was designed so that in the summer months the glass panels on the south side could be removed so as to turn it into an elaborately planted loggia. To avoid spoiling the subtropical effect the hot-water pipes that kept the plants cosy for the winter were uncoupled and like the front glass wall put away out of sight for the summer months. Subtropical plants swagged the rear wall and the stanchions supporting the roof. Many of the other plants were stood about in the decorative pots Johnston collected as he did old tiles and garden seats. Cane furniture helped create a mood of sun-drenched luxury and idleness.

This dream was shattered in the early days of the National Trust's stewardship. Always a man in a hurry to turn his gardening ideas into reality, Johnston had not thought enough about functional security. The rear wall, which was the structure's main

The Plant House has been reconstructed to the original design, as seen in photographs.
A high trellis has been provided for climbing plants to display themselves to full advantage,
while other climbers swag the pillars.

supporting element, was found to be constructed simply with two layers of timber separated by a core of sawdust. The National Trust had to judge it unsafe for a garden open for public viewing and it was demolished.

Many, though, longed to see it created again. More than half a century went by with the Plant House no more than a memory – until a munificent six-figure gift to Hidcote from a well-wisher provided the funds required. Constructed to outlive anyone alive today, the new Plant House was designed to offer the maximum comfort to its plants, which are kept warm in winter and shaded and cooled in high summer by advanced technology. But still the custodian gardeners like to test the soil's moisture content by using sensitive fingertips on the surface or rapping the sides of the clay pots with the knuckles, listening for an answering ring or a sullen thud.

Today the gardeners respectfully style it the tropical shelter. Fortunately, this is one of the areas of the garden of which a detailed inventory was made and still exists, so where possible the plants Johnston cherished there can now be repeated. Most of the pot collection was dispersed but some have been retrieved and others created again at the nearby Whichford Pottery, using old photographs as a pattern book. Just, in fact, as the system of rafters supporting the roof was repeated from indications in a picture.

Along the back wall and on the supporting pillars, twisting and turning according to their nature or trained by the gardeners' understanding fingers or

The Plant House was designed so that the south wall, seen on the left here, could be removed in summer. Repeating some of the plants many times introduces unity to a diverse collection.

secateurs, are many climbing plants. They include the magnificent Burmese *Lonicera hildebrandiana*, finest of all honeysuckles; the yellow-trumpeted *Allamanda*; bougainvilleas; and plumbagos, both the blue and the white kinds, of South African origin. The olives and citrus of southern Europe and the Far East grow here too. Pots stood about in a contrived interior landscape rearranged with the seasons contain ginger plants (hedychiums); the bird of paradise flower (*Strelitzia*); the aptly named *Rhododendron* 'Fragrantissimum'; the *Jasminum polyanthum* today sold in supermarkets in tens of thousands in winter for its clusters of scented flowers; the coral tree (*Erythrina*); and the pot geranium with scented leaves as broad as the palm of your hand and imaginatively named *Pelargonium papilionaceum* – all these and a hundred others redolent of the south where Johnston spent his winters. But perhaps the greatest treasure of all in the Plant House is the waxen-flowered South American *Lapageria rosea*, the Chilean bellflower named after Napoleon's Joséphine, whose maiden name was de la Pagerie and whose original home was on an estate of this name in Martinique.

In the comfort of the Plant House during the winter such plants as this aged silver-variegated agave, stood out of doors from spring onwards till autumn, are saved from the harm wet and chill would cause them.

The approach to the giant borders running the length of the kitchen garden and orchard and planted largely with old shrub roses, known as the Rose Walk (20), is a striking preamble to one of Hidcote's fabled features. Johnston was one of a handful of enthusiasts who in the 1920s and 1930s feared that the shrub roses mostly bred in France in the eighteenth and nineteenth centuries would be lost as raisers of new roses proliferated and produced repeat-flowering kinds more suitable for municipal bedding, which was then being carried out with roses, and for the rose gardens then growing in popularity as design features. It was a time when every garden of any size had to have one of these rose gardens, successors to the beds of greenhouse-raised annual flowers of the late Victorian and Edwardian era, although subsequently they fell from favour as the numbers of professional gardeners on the labour market diminished. Johnson and his associates, notably the designer Norah Lindsay, Maud Messel of Nymans in Sussex and Robert James in Yorkshire, who treasured the historic varieties, sought far and wide for plants of the old shrub roses, or even simply cuttings to root, in order to try to keep them in existence.

For all their variety of form and colouring, the roses – fleeting in flower, one of the weaknesses held against them – do not have the borders to themselves. They are temporarily dominating incidents on a splendid stage. Their background is a series of lilacs now grown to huge size, mostly of the varieties bred – some for their showy double flowers – in the nineteenth century. Beneath is a densely planted groundwork of the spring-flowering soldiers and sailors or pulmonaria.

Four large dome-headed bay trees flank the path to the rose borders. You pass generous plantings of *Viburnum rhytidophyllum*, a fast-growing species with long furry leaves heavily engraved by the veins and silver on the undersides. Then stands, planted centrally, a huge false acacia, a pink-flowered variety, *Robinia hispida* 'Macrophylla'.

At intervals, contrasting in form with the bulky lilacs, are sentinel-like trees of the Irish yew, *Taxus baccata* 'Fastigiata'. By nature this grows in column fashion but acquires obesity with age. The Hidcote trees, however, are clipped in cigar shape. The Irish yew has a most interesting pedigree. Though it is a form of the common yew long planted in churchyards as a symbol of longevity, the years of which can often be

Throughout its length the edges of the Rose Walk are softened by overhanging clumps of the purple-leaved sage, which also contributes to the summer flowering season with its purple spires.

All is white and silver at the north end of the Rose Walk. At high summer regal lilies are a strong element of the composition.

measured in millennia, it was not known until the 1730s, when a tenant farmer found two upright-growing wild yew trees on the Enniskillen estate of Florence Court in the west of Ireland. He dug them up, planted one in his own domain and gave the other to his landlord. The tree he kept died, but his landlord's prospered and became the ancestor of all Irish yews grown ever since. The Florence Court tree, also on National Trust land, lives on still, venerated and visited by dendrologists paying it homage. Left unpruned, it has grown 25 feet/7.5 metres across as more and more branches have added to its girth by first reaching out sideways and then resolutely growing vertically.

The Hidcote old rose collection comprises varieties of the Gallicas, the ancestors of which were said to have been brought from southern Europe by returning Crusaders; the Damasks, recalling in their collective name the old city of Damascus itself; and the Centifolias – 'roses of a hundred leaves' or 'cabbage roses' – as well as roses of the Hybrid Perpetual type, of which thousands were bred in the nineteenth century. Also

the 'white' roses derived from *Rosa × alba*, to the genesis of which our wild hedgerow rose is believed to have contributed; and the Moss roses characterized by the 'moss' with which the elongated calyx of the flower is clad.

What qualities do old roses have which separate them from modern varieties of twentieth-century breeding and which inspired the devotion of a handful of collectors and later brought them into the field of the everyday gardener? The truth is that as the flowers age they develop their characteristic colouring and form, whereas modern roses become untidy in their decline.

Their appeal could be simply their romantic names. Who can resist 'Reine des Violettes', 'Parfum de l'Haÿ', 'Nuits de Young', 'Maiden's Blush', 'Belle de Crécy', 'Tuscany Superb', 'Tricolore de Flandre', 'Cramoisi Supérieur', 'Oeillet Panaché' and 'Cuisse de Nymphe Emué'? Or not wonder who were 'Madame Hardy' and 'Madame Isaac Pereire', 'Ferdinand Pichard', 'William Lobb', 'Madame Lauriol de Barny',

Pillars formed with Irish yews are a unifying element in the rose borders. They are now many years old and their further extension is controlled by hand clipping in early autumn.

'Yvonne Rabier', 'Louis Gimard', 'Henri Martin' and – creeping into this distinguished company as though by a side door – 'Agnes Griffiths', all honoured imperishably with having roses named after them?

Most of the Hidcote roses bloom in one glorious midsummer burst and then sink into obscurity until the next year. Tulips in generous clumps, lupins and patches of alpine auriculas precede them while we await the great moment of the roses. As these retire, ceanothus of the large-leaved deciduous type take up the relay. As well as the blue varieties named 'Henri Desfossé' and 'Indigo', they come in pink in 'Ceres', 'Perle Rose' and 'Marie Simon'. Soon it is time for many kinds of penstemons, which prove hardy in the root-threaded, well-drained soil here and dangle their bell-shaped flowers from gently arching stems. The flowering season is brought to an end by the appearance of many Japanese anemones. Soon all is left to the architectural forms of the Irish yews and the foreground clumps of sage holding on to their aromatic leaves of silvery jade, purple, gold or, in the case of the 'painted variety', pink, purple and cream.

LEFT A striking example of the rare *Wisteria floribunda* 'Alba' enshrines the white-painted seat at the northern end of the Rose Walk.

RIGHT, ABOVE *Tulipa orphanidea* Whittallii Group, rarely seen in gardens, is one of the many species and cultivars of tulip which remain favourites in the garden, even though they have to be replaced often.

RIGHT, BELOW *Rosa* 'Nuits de Young' is one of the old roses in the collection with an intriguing name.

A single tree of great distinction dominates the richly planted Garden Yard (21): *Davidia involucrata* var. *vilmoriniana*, the ghost, dove or handkerchief tree. In flower it is arresting but the display is made not by the flowers themselves but by the large white papery bracts that hang below them, giving rise to the three common names. In its generic name it honours the earliest of those Jesuit missionaries who went out to China from France and who were naturalists as well as priests, Père Jean Pierre Armand David (1826–1900). He found the tree in 1869, but it was not until 1897 that seed was sent home, by another missionary, Paul Guillaume Farges (1844–1912). Of the thirty-seven seeds sent – the seeds are hard nuts, like almonds – only one germinated at the nursery of the Vilmorin seed firm near Paris. The resulting tree flowered first in 1906.

Meanwhile, intrigued by reports of this wondrous tree, the English nursery firm of Veitch despatched E.H. Wilson (1876–1930), who later became one of the most successful plant collectors of all time, to western China to bring back seed. Wilson had been born near Hidcote at Chipping Campden, was apprenticed at a nursery near by and later studied at the Royal Botanic Gardens, Kew. He returned not only with the davidia seed in such quantity that 13,000 plants were raised from it but also with seed of more than 300 other species, together with 35 cases of bulbs and roots of plants. Veitch sent him back two years later, and he made several further expeditions to the Far East, sponsored by the Arnold Arboretum at Washington, only to be killed eventually in a car crash in the United States, the country of his adoption.

The Veitch name is commemorated in many plants, including the hydrangea in the Courtyard. The firm had a long record of sponsoring plant collecting trips and established nurseries for exotic indoor plants and trees and shrubs. One branch of the family continued in business at Exeter, but the branch that brought the name its greatest fame, establishing nurseries in the Home Counties, with one member of the family receiving a knighthood, closed down in 1914.

The west-facing shop wall has a series of interesting plants trained to shelter against it. Acacia-like in its feathery leaves, *Robinia kelseyi* has clusters of lilac-pink flowers, and there is a remarkable bramble here, *Rubus ulmifolius* 'Bellidiflorus', which has double pink flowers that come out as summer begins to wane. The largest plant in the grouping

Country crafts still practised in the Cotswolds are represented by this artistic thatching on one of Hidcote's outbuildings.

here is another of the climbing hydrangea family, a relative of that already seen on the chapel, *Schizophragma integrifolium*. It is even more splendid when carrying its display of bracts surrounding its insignificant flowers.

The other tree in the yard is a singular Japanese flowering cherry, which bears the name 'Ukon', the word for yellowish in its native country. This is indeed a flowering cherry with yellow flowers, the only such variety ever seen in Britain. It is enhanced by the copper tint of the unfolding leaves at the same time that the large double flowers are at their best.

The rose on the house wall with flowers of buff yellow that open from copper buds and highly polished leaves is 'Rêve d'Or', which dates back to 1860. It is one of the Noisettes, the first of which was raised by a nurseryman of Charleston, South Carolina, Philippe Noisette, setting a new standard for climbing roses that flower repeatedly through the summer instead of in one glorious June burst.

More interesting climbing plants grow against the west end of the house walls and its outbuildings. *Actinidia kolomikta* is the strangest, with parti-coloured leaves, the green tipped with pink overlying white. *Jasminum × stephanense* is a summer jasmine with plentiful pink, not white, flowers, and *Lonicera × americana* is one of the most splendid of the honeysuckles with scented flowers that are white when they open, turn cream and then deep yellow as they age, when purplish tones are prominent on the outsides. But if it is early June it will be the splendid wisteria covering the roof of one of the outbuildings that takes the eye most.

ABOVE Tender plants used in summer plantings return to the greenhouses and outbuildings for winter.

OPPOSITE The gates from the Garden Yard are in the pattern of originals at Cleeve Priory, Worcestershire.

ENVOI

Not until you are about to leave the garden do you experience Hidcote's second most thrilling moment. Now you understand why the main entrance gates are set so oddly, at an angle to the approach road instead of breasting the courtyard full face on as you would expect. As you reach the twin stone piers capped with elegant finials, you are suddenly stopped in your tracks – not to take a last look back but by the view lying immediately in front of you.

An avenue made of tall holly hedges running a hundred yards or more concentrates the distant scene. The perspective is emphasized by tall cedars to the left and pines to the right, as the ilex trees did in the Long Walk, standing behind those hornbeam hedges. This is the prelude to another succeeding avenue, this time of deciduous trees, running several hundred yards further this time – right, it seems, to the horizon. The two in combination frame the northern sky in the distance. You feel as if you are catching a glimpse of the very edge of the world, for there at the end of this great vista is no stone eyecatcher or tree posed in silhouette but just the sky.

Once the trees here were parallel lines of elms, their tall, bald trunks supporting arching branches. They were like the vaulted nave of some immense Gothic cathedral, but greater than any ever built. They were elms of the specially tall Huntingdon type, *Ulmus* × *vegeta*, given its common name from the fact that it came from a nursery in Huntingdon in the middle of the eighteenth century. This native hybrid was noted for the fashion in which the branches spread – making the ribs of the 'vaulting' on this occasion. Alas, the trees fell victim to the Dutch elm disease brought to Britain early in the 1970s on timber imported from Canada, which destroyed millions of elms throughout the country. Now the place of the dramatic Hidcote planting, remembered honourably in photographs, has been taken by trees of the common lime, *Tilia* × *europaea*.

The whole of the outside wall of the courtyard and chapel is festooned with a variegated ivy, *Hedera helix* 'Angularis Aurea'. The yellow splashed on the leaves is picked up by the summer-long yellow flowers of the rose of Sharon, *Hypericum calycinum*, which has suckered voluminously to make a ribbon at the foot.

Opposite, even the farmyard walls are gardened. They play host to two curiously named climbing roses, 'Blairii Number One' and 'Blairii Number Two'. Each carrying

Heavy timber gates seal off Hidcote Manor Garden from the world beyond, enclosing an idealized paradise.

flattened soft pink roses of the old-fashioned type, they are said to have been raised in the 1840s by a Thomas Blair at Stamford Hill, north London, who presumably couldn't think up suitable names for them. In few other gardens is he recalled.

Inevitably you are led to explore the road, where a handful of trim cottages come into view. Almost at once yet another great vista is revealed. Commanded by the upper windows of the house, it strides across the field opposite right to the foot of the hill that finally encloses the scene. On this occasion the avenue of trees is broad and composed of twin lines of the common lime, *Tilia* × *europaea*.

This is the only one of Hidcote's major vistas that is focused on an eyecatcher in the distance. A giant figure of Hercules, a classical reproduction, stands on his plinth there, framed by the clean trunks of the limes and against a background of turf and trees. A ha-ha prevents you from approaching.

There is no attempt at concealment or jealous guarding of privacy – part of Hidcote's prevailing character – about the siting of the Lime Avenue. It is extrovert and open to the public road into the hamlet for all to see, an indelible part of the landscape surrounding the garden. The spirit of privacy returns, however, in the last view of Hidcote as you leave by the road running west along the north side of the garden. After a few yards you stop beside a pair of timber gates of the same pattern and painted the same slate blue as the courtyard gates and the doors of the outbuildings, which you did not notice on your arrival. These gates lead directly into the leafy darkness of the avenues through the beech wood that you glimpsed from the Theatre Lawn. You can just see the clean line of the clipped yew hedge that encloses that great expanse of mown turf. Rising above this dark wall is the pointed roof of the north gazebo. The padlock and chain emphasize that behind it there is a private, intimate world. A fragment of paradise, perhaps? Certainly there is magic beyond those locked blue gates. Having just experienced it, a first-time Hidcote visitor said to me, 'Once you've been here you can never be the same again.'

In the French style the Lime Avenue opposite the front of the Manor is one of Hidcote's few vistas focused on an eyecatcher – in this case a stone figure of Hercules.

SERRE *de la* MADONE

For nearly forty years Lawrence Johnston's other garden in the south of France remained as reclusive as the man. Yet it was created with the same genius for design and zest for collecting plants and setting them with a faultless touch in an environment congenial to them, both at the root and in the effect they make. Now it has been restored and given a foundation that will ensure its preservation.

The garden lies on a steep hillside just north-west of the town of Menton, in a small area known to have the mildest climate of the whole of the Riviera, though it is a little colder than gardens close to the sea. Johnston bought the site in 1924. For a man of piety as well as unquenchable zeal for horticulture, it was fortunate that it was named Serre de la Madone. Johnston added two wings to the old farmhouse and gradually acquired more land until the garden spread over 17 acres/7 hectares. Over the next twenty-five years he expended his passions upon it, working a magic the garden retains to this day, in spite of trees having soared far beyond the scale envisaged at the outset, because of the mild climate. An inventory compiled by a botanist containing the names of several hundred plants.

Facing south-west, at moments offering glimpses of the sea, the land had once been devoted to the region's twin crops of olives and grapes, and was already terraced with retaining walls that had held the earth fast against centuries of tempests that in a night can wrench it from the rock that lies close beneath. The rainfall was high for a sunny place, as much as 50 inches/1.25 metres in a year, but mostly coming in autumn and early spring.

By the time he bought Serre de la Madone the prentice hand Johnston had worked with at Hidcote had become accomplished. As he transformed the Provençal-type farmhouse into a gracious home he refashioned twenty-two terraces and embellished them with the same flair and inventiveness he had revealed at Hidcote, each given its own planting scheme. Of course he had help, as at Hidcote. He acknowledged it by placing a memorial table on one of the stone clematis pillars to his first head gardener there, Henry Lloyd, who died during service in the garden.

The terraced garden at Serre de la Madone, Lawrence Johnston's other garden in the south of France, enjoys many weeks of dryness and sunshine in the year, but also a high winter rainfall which fills the cisterns from which the plants are watered in summer.

Replacements of the original green glazed vases, planted with dwarf orange trees and made in the Provençal pottery town of Anduze, are part of the restoration of the garden carried out over five years. Each bears the initials 'LJ' in a cartouche.

The sense of theatre is there immediately you step inside the gates. The drive takes a serpentine course up the hillside, lined with cypress trees and spiky yuccas planted alternately for contrast of form. A large-leaved *Magnolia delavayi*, usually planted against walls – as in the Hidcote Courtyard – grows as a free-standing tree, one of a large collection of this genus; winter jasmines and a Banksian rose reaches through it towards the open sky. Flower beds spurt extravagant plantings of blue South African agapanthus and the Mexican beschorneria, most splendid of foliage plants.

Close to the house the walls are draped with sweet-smelling *Trachelospermum*. On my first visit there in 1953 a night-flowering cereus – the very same plant pictured in the famous Thornton's Temple of Flora plate – flourished in the reflected heat of the wall and close to it, reaching up to the eaves, was a *Hibiscus rosa-sinensis* intertwined with the splendid purple trumpet vine, *Thunbergia grandiflora*. Two paved gardens, one a little above the other, run away from the southern end of the villa. In one, an area for outdoor meals and lounging in the mid-winter sun, the floor is a pattern worked in pebbles, in the ancient style. The other has a loggia for shade, from which you can watch the doves flying in and out of the columbarium at the other end and admire the

The plant house overlooking the mirror pool serves as a loggia for very tender plants in summer and acts as an orangery in the cooler months. Nelumbiums, or sacred lotus, are in the foreground.

repeated planting of bird of paradise plants, the South African strelitzias, set against the topmost retaining wall.

On the twenty-two terraces Johnston made pools and fountains. He planted them lavishly with collections of proteas, tree peonies, mimosas, cistus and ceanothus. He scattered them with the tricky bulbs of the Eastern Mediterranean-like tulip species. He planted trees such as the Australian melaleucas and the tender, highly perfumed *Osmanthus fragrans*. He imported tender camellias from Japan and interplanted them with gardenia bushes. Also from Japan came wisterias otherwise unknown in Europe. Imaginative interplanting was something he did with an individual flair. Pink belladonna lilies danced above a carpet of blue hardy plumbago; in a box-edged parterre striped 'lady tulips', *Tulipa clusiana*, rose from a groundwork of double-flowered periwinkle.

The broadest terrace is almost filled with a huge rectangular pool, empty of plants and a mirror to the sky. In another nearby pool, of crescent shape, grow papyrus plants, 8 feet/2.5 metres tall, and in yet another sacred lotus, their leaves a couple of feet across and the pink flower heads poised well above the water. Placed around the edges of the terrace are great vases d'Anduze, a set of eighteenth-century green glazed urns, in

A wisteria overhangs and shades an ironwork rotunda which commands a view across the pool and many of the terraces, as well as the villa, against which exotic climbers are trained.

which grow dwarf citrus trees. At the opposite end stands a plant house, where still more exotic plants grow. The garden also has such conceits as a wisteria-clad rotunda, a hilltop belvedere commanding a view away towards the sea, and a huge area wired in as an aviary. Johnston had a close affinity with birds and his aviary was home to many exotic species. He also had a family of macaws flying free and trained to return to their perches close to the villa. A pair of Pyrenean mountain dogs, called Pax and Zephyr, lolled about on the terraces.

When Johnston died, his heir, Nancy Lindsay, a well-known plantswoman who had collected in Persia and was the daughter of Norah Lindsay, sold the villa, having first invited the Cambridge Botanic Garden to take whatever plants could be moved or scions from those too old to suffer this. The treasure they garnered included *Mahonia siamensis*, until then not known in Britain; it has orange flowers and the largest leaves of the whole *Mahonia* genus. Some of the statuary was sold off, together with the handsome green glazed vases d'Anduze.

What happened to Serre de la Madone eventually? Speculators bought it as a

possible building site, but the local council demurred. Agitation grew. The cry went out: 'Serre de la Madone must be preserved!' But how? Events took a remarkable turn when the Ministry for Culture up in Paris declared it a *monument historique*. This was the first time the appellation had been conferred on a French garden in its own right. After prolonged negotiation it was entrusted to the care of the Conservatoire du Littoral who instituted a five-year restoration project. It has now become one of the gardens managed by the city of Menton and is open to visitors from the end of April to the end of October. In fine order again, it is also one of the overseas gardens that can be visited by members of the Royal Horticultural Society on production of a membership card.

Today the magnolia trees soar still higher. The Banksian roses reach 30 feet/9 metres into the heads of the cypresses. The winter irises edging the terrace beds would need an axe to divide them; plantings of agapanthus and beschorneria would defy fork or spade. When restoration began, some of the paths were blocked by the exuberant bushes. But the Serre de la Madone garden retains its magic under its new carers, who have the means and the zeal to recapture the freshness its originality once gave it.

The beds of a box-edged parterre are thickly planted, in the Johnstonian style, with bulbs of the cherry and white striped 'lady tulip', *Tulipa clusiana*, which have seeded themselves prodigally.

INDEX

Note: Page numbers in **bold** type refer to the main entries for named areas of the garden and include illustrations on those pages. Page numbers in *italic* refer to all other illustrations.

ACKNOWLEDGEMENTS

My thanks are due to Mike Beeston, Property Manager at Hidcote, and Glynn Jones, Head Gardener there, also members of their staff, who have generously shared with me their deep knowledge and unbounded enthusiasm for the garden. I owe inestimable thanks to Anne Fraser, who commissioned the project; to Jo Christian, who skilfully piloted it at all stages; Anne Askwith, who edited my copy; and art director Becky Clarke, who designed the book.

Martin Smith, connoisseur of Riviera gardens, supplied the photographs of Serre de la Madone and guided me through the complicated process of restoration and trusteeship there.

Finally, I must pay a grateful tribute to my wife, Pat, who from the time I made my first revelatory visit to Hidcote in 1949 has patiently and encouragingly endured my unceasing chatter about it and my zeal for gaining intimacy with the garden and attempting a pen portrait of its creator. *FW*

PHOTOGRAPHIC ACKNOWLEDGEMENTS

With the exception of those listed below, all photographs in this book are copyright © Tony Lord
Courtesy of the National Trust: 29, 44
Courtesy of Martin Smith: 22, 148–153
Courtesy of Serre de la Madone: 21